Listening
to a Pogrom
on the Radio

Listening
to a Pogrom
on the Radio
Michael Rosen

STACK
BOOKS

Smokestack Books
1 Lake Terrace, Grewelthorpe, Ripon HG4 3BU
e-mail: info@smokestack-books.co.uk
www.smokestack-books.co.uk

ISBN 9780995767522

Smokestack Books
is represented
by Inpress Ltd

Contents

The Dentist and the Toe

I was at the dentist and when he had finished
I said, One of my toes is hurting, could you
take a look at it while I'm here?
He said, Sure.
I took off my shoes and socks and he looked
closely at the toe I was talking about.
He said, I can do a variety of things here, I
can drill down behind the nail and then give you
a temporary filling; I could take a mould, then
remove the toe and give you a new toe; or
I could send you to a chiropodist.
I said, I like the sound of the new toe.
So he said, Fine and got to work straightaway.
It all went fine. This was a few weeks ago
and I've got the new toe. It's OK – not great
though. It's a bit inflexible because it's made
of the stuff they fill teeth with. I was talking to
someone the other day about it, and she said
that all I had probably needed to do was
cut my nails a bit more carefully.

Look Right

When you see the sign 'Look right'
don't make the mistake of looking to your right.
It refers to the fact that you need to smarten up.

Sign

When you see the sign 'Help point'
it means
Help!
Point!

Christmas Cake

My German Christmas cake has gone.
Stollen.

Spam

I got some spam mail from someone called Elite Chairs.
In the field it said, 'Are you sitting down?'
Wrong question to ask surely.
If they want to sell me a chair, shouldn't they be asking,
'Are you standing up?'

Storage

Remember,
from now on much of your stuff will be in storage,
while you and your loved ones convince each other that one
day it'll 'come out of storage'. It won't.

Life is storage.

There was a time when I thought Sartre had something useful
to say but he didn't talk about storage.
He thought being was doing.
He didn't realise that being is storing.
And big bloody yellow storage people are better philosophers
than Sartre.
They realised that because people want to be attached to more
than they have room for, they'll pay big yellow storage people
money forever.

Being is storing, Jean-Paul.

Suitcase

for the family while sitting in airport waiting rooms

I'm a suitcase
in the attic all year
I'm a suitcase
stuffed full of gear
I'm a suitcase
crammed in a hold
I'm a suitcase
freezing cold

Well yes...

I may be a suitcase
but I want to be free
I want to go to the beach,
and swim in the sea
I want to go to the mountains
and learn how to ski
I want to hear music
dance and shout
You leave me in the room
when you go out.
But I don't want to be baggage
It's not what I want to be.
I'm a suitcase
and I want to be free.

Next trip you take
you're in for a shock
I may be quiet
shut tight with a lock
But while you're out
enjoying the sun
I'll escape
I'll be on the run
A suitcase on the move
looking for fun.
I'll be that suitcase
Yes, that'll be me
I'm a suitcase
who wants to be free.

Sour Milk

My mother ate sour milk.
We didn't have a fridge.
The milk was in the larder.
And sometimes it went sour.
When my brother and I came down to breakfast,
if the milk was sour, we tipped it down the sink.
It was blobby and when it came out of the bottle
it went ker-plup, ker-plup, ker-plup
and dribbly stuff flowed out too.
But it was the smell.
You couldn't put your face over the sink
while the sour milk was coming out.
It was worse than sick.
And it made you want to be sick.

If my mother was there though
she'd say, 'Oh don't throw that away,'
and she poured the sour milk into a bowl
and ate it with a spoon.
It was like she was eating white sick.

My brother and I said,
'Nooooooo! You can't. That's horrible.'
'Mmmm, lovely,' she said
and you could hear her sipping it.
Sip, sip, sip.

She tried to get us to understand.
'You know the nursery rhyme about Little Miss Muffet,'
she said. 'Curds and whey'? That's what this is,' she said.
'We don't care,' we said, 'it's horrible.'

Our dad explained that Mum's grandfather
made yoghurt and something called
'shmatana' and sour milk.
It didn't make it any better.
Why would anyone make sour milk?

When we went to see Mum's mother,
she gave us shmatana.
That was nice.
She didn't try the sour milk on us though.
Just as well.

Chulent

Every now and then
my father would look into the distance
and say, 'My Bubbe's chulent.'
(We never had 'chulent'. We never saw 'chulent'.
We didn't know what 'chulent' was.)
Mum would say, 'Why do you keep going on about
your Bubbe's "chulent"? I'm not going to make "chulent".
I'm not going to stand in the kitchen for a whole day
making "chulent".
If you want "chulent", make your own "chulent".
Don't keep going on about "chulent". Just because
your Bubbe made you "chulent" doesn't mean
that I'm going to make you "chulent".'

But it was as if he didn't hear a word she said.
He just went on looking into the distance,
thinking of his Bubbe's 'chulent'.

A few months would go by.
We wouldn't hear about Bubbe's 'chulent' in that time
then one day we'd be sitting having a meal
he'd look into the distance and say,
'My Bubbe's chulent.'
And Mum would say,
'Why do you keep going on about
your Bubbe's "chulent"? I'm not going to make "chulent".
I'm not going to stand in the kitchen for a whole day
making "chulent".
If you want "chulent", make your own "chulent".
Don't keep going on about "chulent". Just because
your Bubbe made you "chulent" doesn't mean
I'm going to make you "chulent".'

And it was if he didn't hear a word she said.
He just went on looking into the distance,
thinking of his Bubbe's chulent.

A few months would go by
We wouldn't hear about Bubbe's chulent in that time
then we'd be sitting having a meal,
he'd look into the distance and say
'My Bubbe's chulent.'
And Mum would...

Prunes

Every now and then
my father would look into the distance
and say, 'My Bubbe's prunes.
You don't see prunes like that anymore, you know.
They were huge. And so juicy.
Prunes nowadays are small, dry and hard.
These were giant prunes. You could hardly get
one in your mouth. That's how big they were.'
And Mum would say, 'These are the prunes we've got.
These are the only prunes there are.
If you don't like them, don't eat them.
No one's going to make you eat them.'
and he would say,
'My Bubbe's prunes.
You don't see prunes like that anymore, you know.
They were huge. And so juicy.
Prunes nowadays are small, dry and hard.
These were giant prunes. You could hardly get
one in your mouth. That's how big they were.'

A few months would go by
then one day my father would look into the distance
and say, 'My Bubbe's prunes.
You don't see prunes like that anymore, you know.
They were huge. And so juicy.
Prunes nowadays are small, dry and hard.
These were giant prunes. You could hardly get
one in your mouth. That's how big they were.'
And Mum would say, 'These are the prunes we've got.
These are the only prunes there are.
If you don't like them, don't eat them.
No one's going to make you eat them.'
and he would say,
'My Bubbe's prunes.
You don't see prunes like that anymore, you know.
They were huge. And so juicy.
Prunes nowadays are small, dry and hard.

These were giant prunes. You could hardly get
one in your mouth. That's how big they were.'

Then a few months would go by
and one day my father would look into the distance
and say, 'My Bubbe's prunes...'

Because My Parents Were Communists

Because my parents were Communists
I thought everything they did was Communist.
Not just going to Trafalgar Square
or holding branch meetings in our front room.
Not just shouting at Anthony Eden on the radio
or crying about the Spanish Civil War.
I mean everything.
Like camping, or Marmite.
Camping was definitely Communist
because we went with other Communists.
Marmite was Communist because Mum said it was good for us.
They liked going into old churches
and my father especially liked old walls.
He loved an old wall.
He knew a poem about an old wall
and sometimes he said it out loud.
Old walls must have been pretty Communist too.
They said they thought the butcher
we went to was very good.
I once heard them recommend him
to some Communist friends of theirs
so he must have been a Communist butcher
until one day I was playing football
with the butcher's son and he said
that his dad said that we should drop the bomb on Russia.
Later, much later,
things got much more complicated.
Especially when my mother said,
'I think I'm an anarcho-Stalinist'.

Who was a Communist?

My parents didn't tell us which of their friends and relations
were Communists and which weren't,
so we had to figure it out for ourselves.

A group of teachers and their partners came over
from my father's school,
Len got out his guitar and they sang,
'I'm the man, the very fat man who waters the workers' beer'.
They must be Communists, I thought.

A group of teachers came over from my mother's school,
and a man called Wally told stories about an engraving firm
controlled by 'the masons', he said.
My dad was fascinated by Wally's stories and kept saying,
'Christ, would you believe it?!'
So I asked my mum if Wally was a Communist
and she said, 'Of course not, you mustn't ever say that.'

Then we went on a camp with the Hornsey Communists
and a woman spilt meths on her groundsheet
and it burst in to flame.
My dad said she was a bloody fool
so I reckoned that though she might have been a
Communist once
she wasn't one now.

We went camping with Fred and Lorna,
and when we sang 'I'm the man the very fat man
who waters the workers' beer' Lorna didn't join in
and said, 'Oh Fred, come on, there's no need to
sing that one', so Lorna, I thought, was not very Communist.

Sometimes we went to see two families who
lived upstairs and downstairs in a house.

Upstairs was Francis the Armenian who was so Communist
quite often he wasn't there – he was working for peace
in Czechoslovakia. Peggy, his wife, though
was very Communist, I thought, because
she not only talked about peace, she talked about
peace-loving peoples.

My father said that she sounded like a bloody gramophone
record, but as we often used to listen to bloody gramophone
records of the Red Army, I didn't know why there
could be anything wrong with that.

Downstairs there was Roy who was the most miserable
man I have ever known. Even his hands was miserable.
He said that everything was bad. As my parents
said some things (but not everything) were bad as well,
it was possible, I thought,
Roy was more Communist than them.

Roy's wife, was sometimes ill and had to go to bed for
months. But when she came out of the bedroom
she was very smiley and seemed to say that
everything wasn't as bad as Roy said it was.
I wasn't sure if that meant she was more or less
Communist than Roy.

There was Moishe and Rene who weren't just
Communists they were almost my parents.
Moishe went to school with my father and
Rene went to school with my mother.
They had even camped together.

When they talked it was like they were
a moishe-rene-my mother-my father Communist camping club.

Then there were the relatives or 'meshpukkhe' as
my father called them.
My father's mother was so old and so Communist, she was the
first Communist. And her father they said, was a
Communist-before-there-even-were-Communists.

My mother's mother, 'Bubbe', kept
chickens and said the woman who did the 'bag wash'
was trying to diddle her. My father said that she
wasn't a Communist, she just 'kvetshed' (complained)
but she made the best shmatena (a kind of yoghurt)
in London so maybe that made her some kind of
a Communist without knowing she was.

I asked my mother if 'Zeyde' (her father) was a
Communist and she said very angrily that he was
'some kind of Trotskyist'.
That sounded terrible. And yet he was so nice.
He took me to Hackney Downs where he
showed me to his friends who said, every time,
'Is that your Grandson, Frank?'
'Yes,' he said every time,
'He's a nice looking boy,' they said every time,
and went on talking in Yiddish.
As I didn't speak Yiddish I had no way of knowing
whether they were Trotskyists too.

In 1957, we went to Communist East Germany
and there was a row between everybody on the
delegation about whether Stalinallee (Stalin Alley)
looked like a public lavatory or not.
We saw the Carl Zeiss camera works,
Frederick the Great's house,
Goethe's house, Schiller's house, Bach's house,
Luther's castle, Buchenwald concentration camp
and Hitler's bunker.

When we got back, my parents stopped being Communists.
They called me and my brother in and said
that they didn't agree with the Communist Party and democracy.
I had no idea what that meant. Not a clue.
Some of the ones who were Communists went on being
Communists and now we weren't Communists.

Every so often Roy came over and said
everything was getting worse.

People Run

People run away from war:
my father's uncle and his wife
ran away from war.
They ran from one side of France to another.
But the authorities divided people up:
some who ran away were good;
some, like my father's uncle and his wife,
were not so good:
they were not born in France.
So they were put on a list
and had everything taken away from them.
They heard that people like them were
being put on trains and sent away to the east.
So they escaped and ran across France
again.
This was a good move,
they were safe now,
all they had to do was wait.
While they were waiting
the authorities in this place got defeated,
they were seized, put on a train
put in a transit camp, then on another train
to another camp,
where they were killed.
People run away from war.
Sometimes we get away.
Sometimes we don't.
Sometimes we're helped.
Sometimes we aren't.

The Migrants in Me

Don't think you can take the migrants out of me.
Every time I hear you say all the wrongs that
migrants supposedly do,
you are saying it to the migrants in me,
people who travelled thousands of miles
so they could work in sweat shops,
in boot and shoe factories, on market stalls,
people who ran from danger, threats, hate,
bullets and bombs.

Maybe I look as if you could take the migrants
out of me,
my hands are soft,
no one's told me I'm not allowed to live here
though someone once told me I'm not
'indigenous',
which made me wonder: if I'm not indigenous,
are my children indigenous?
Would their children be indigenous?
When does a person become indigenous?
How long does it take to be indigenous?

Maybe I look as if you can spin a story at me
about how threatening and dangerous
migrants are,
as if neither I nor you would ever dream
of upping sticks and living somewhere else
and being, you know,
a migrant,
as if neither I nor you might suddenly
find ourselves in a wrong place at a wrong time
carrying the wrong passport,
with a face that doesn't fit,
and needing to get out, move, find a safe place
because, what is it, only mad, bad and sad people
do that sort of thing
and neither me or you are mad, bad or sad enough?

so, don't think you can take the migrants out of me;
the migrants in me tell me about
criss-crossing Europe
criss-crossing the Atlantic
they warn me,
they remind me of
long, long hours at work benches,
they remind me of relatives,
who at one moment, were as safe as houses,
and the next had no houses to be safe in
who fled armies, officials, police,
all acting legally on behalf of their governments,
relatives who found themselves
sitting ducks
waiting to be snaffled, transported,
and disappeared forever,
and of course you don't want anything
like that to happen to anyone
even though our country
acting in our name
has helped in the business of turning
millions out of their houses
people so desperate
as to climb into rubber dinghies
as if they were as safe as houses.

Migration

Our governments migrate bombs
but they don't call that migration.
Our governments migrate drones
but they don't call that migration
Our governments migrate bullets
but they don't call that migration.
Our governments migrate war
but they don't call that migration.
Our banks migrate money
but they don't call that migration
Our banks migrate billions
but they don't call that migration.
business migrates jobs
but they don't call that migration
All these people migrate misery
but they don't call that migration.
We say no to blaming migrants
we say no to racism
no to blaming migrants
no to racism.

I Was Listening to a Pogrom on the Radio Today

I was listening to a pogrom on the radio today
coming from a party conference where they had a lot to say
about people who move, people who move here
and I got it from the pogrom this is something to fear
I should worry about the people next door
I should worry about the woman cleaning the floor
I should worry about the student on the bus
I should worry about anyone moving amongst us
I got it from the pogrom we need more checking
I got it from the pogrom we need more inspecting
'cos any troubles we have, any troubles we know
never come from the people running the show
let's put our hands together and please give thanks
to the people we trust – like those running banks
please give thanks to those who own stocks and shares
they're the ones we can trust to wipe away our cares

I was listening to a pogrom on the radio today
it sounded more like a programme coming our way
a programme, a plan, a strategy, a dream
a way of building up an idea of a nation
based on selection and segregation.
I know going on about it makes me sound like a bore
but, tell me, haven't we heard this sort of thing before?

Concerns about Immigration

The media keep saying:

'People are expressing concerns about immigration
People are expressing concerns about immigration
People are expressing concerns about immigration'

If you are registered as non-dom you can run a business
in the UK but pay no tax. This costs us billions.

'People are expressing concerns about immigration.'

If the government cuts public services, they increase
pressure on public services.

'People are expressing concerns about immigration.'

Since 1980, wealth has shifted from labour to capital.
In other words those that 'have', have more; those that
have the least, have less. Those that have the least
have given wealth to those that have more.

'People are expressing concerns about immigration'

The government regularly announces that it freezes
the wages of public service workers. This means that
people can afford less. Their living standards decline.

'People are expressing concerns about immigration'

The government has repeatedly brought in policies
which have helped to increase the price of houses.
The proportion of people's income required to rent or buy
has steadily risen. Flats and houses cost more to live in.
There is less space per pound of people's income.

'People are expressing concerns about immigration'

Some people do not know that the main reasons for their
standard of living to go down are nothing to do with
immigration.
Instead, they keep hearing:

'People are expressing concerns about immigration.'

You know what happens next?

some people express some concern about immigration.
After all, people can only think what they think
based on available information.
The media supply the available information.
They keep saying:

'People are expressing concerns about immigration.'

The government laughs quietly to itself:
'People do not blame us for their living standards going down,
they blame immigration.'

Lists

Lists
Lists of foreigners
Lists of foreign born people
living and working alongside
those not on lists
Lists of children sitting alongside
children not on lists
Lists to be sent in to government
departments
Lists of names, addresses that can
pass from official to official
from department to department
so that what starts out as 'information'
drifts into ways of saying to those
on the lists that they should have less
they should have no guarantees of the
right to work or live alongside or amongst
those not on the lists.
And when it comes to a time when
those who want to say that hard times
are not the fault of people in government
and not the fault of those who own and control
everything
the lists are ready and waiting.
Look who's on the lists, they'll say
The lists say it all, they'll say.

Le Front National

Enfant de Vichy,
la dernière fois que tu était le gouvernement
tu as donné l'adresse de mon grand-oncle et tante
aux Nazis.
Comme ça, les Nazis les ont trouvés et déportés
à Auschwitz d'où ils ne sont pas rentrés.

Quels plans as-tu cette fois-ci?

The National Front

Child of Vichy
the last time you were the government
you gave my great-uncle and aunt's address
to the Nazis.
That was how the Nazis found them and deported them
to Auschwitz, from where they never came back.

What are your plans this time?

Immigrants

When the government made people have self-employed contracts (thereby taking them off benefits but they were still on low income), immigrants issued that government command.

When New Labour and the Tories let zero hour working expand, that was because a flood of immigrants created zero hour contracts.

When Alan Johnson said containerisation in the docks made thousands unemployed, he meant to say that thousands of immigrants closed the docks.

When Nick Clegg said in 2015 that the Coalition had frozen public sector wages, he meant to say floods of migrants froze them.

The reason why unemployment shot up in Dagenham a few years ago was because thousands of immigrants surrounded Fords and closed it.

And it was immigrants who crashed the banks in 2008 and forced the government to bail them out... and then made us pay for the bail out.

That's immigrants for you.

There's One!

Last night,
scene at the waiting bay for getting on
the cross-channel ferry at Caen:
two young black men walk between the cars
lined up waiting to board the boat.
Two police officers appear and a moment later
are seen walking one of the men away.
People from two of the cars –
one French, the other English –
jump up and shout to the police that
there was 'another one'.
They point in the direction that the two men went.
Everyone else sits tight.
Later on, the police search several camper cars
to see if anyone has attempted to get on board any of them.

I'm left thinking about the reflex of the people in the cars
leaping up and saying to the police,
'There's another one! Over there!'

Refugee Problem Solved

'Hey you! Are you on your own?
Do. You. Understand. Me?
Mmm?
How old are you? What? What? Fine.
But are you on your own?
Right. Good.
I'm going to give you an arm band.
Hold your arm still. That means you're coming with us.
You're going to be very happy.
People will take photos of you.
Make sure you look at the camera and smile.
It's very important that you smile.
And good people are going to meet you when we get to Britain.
One of them is called David.
David Cameron.
Make sure you smile when you meet him.
That's very important.
Remember:
look happy whenever any of us get anywhere near you.
Do you like Haribo sweets?
Good. Here's one.
Keep the armband on, OK?'

Blame

Pause a moment
politician, journalist.
Think of the times you have
hinted or suggested or stated
that the problem yes the problem
is foreigners, migrants, immigrants, refugees.
Think of the times you have hinted
or suggested or stated
that hard times were caused by the people you call
foreigners, migrants, immigrants, refugees,
as if hard times were not caused by
bankers gambling with trillions,
not caused by governments
deliberately holding down pay
and sacking people or cutting
social services public services
and the health service.
Think of those times that you thought you could shore up your position,
garner more support,
get more power by saying these things,
using the excuse you are 'listening to peoples concerns',
the very concerns you stirred with your headlines and speeches
which blamed foreigners for people's hard times,
rather than your own part in the shenanigans
that let the bankers run off with billions,
or the government say that the people had to pay for that
with their wages, and how chasing tax avoiders is too, too difficult.
And just watch what you unleash.
See what voices rise to the surface after your hints and suggestions:
people emboldened by what you said,
People emboldened to put forward plans to
dismiss, fire, exile, intern, detain, deport.
And in so doing win and use powers to
control, contain, restrict, deprive, intern, detain everyone.
That's how it works: blame 'the other' to control all.

Blame the other to control all.

Security Alert

Before you read this
I have to ask you some questions:
Could you tell me if you are any of the following:
migrant, immigrant, refugee, asylum seeker, emigre,
clandestine, *sans papiers*, foreigner,
or a son or daughter of any of the above
or if you LOOK like as if you could be any of the above?
In which case please
state your name, date of birth,
height, weight, inside leg measurement, blood group, hospital records,
skin colour, income,
preferred sandwich type.

Are you are in receipt of any loans or any imported meat products?
Do you intend to stay in this country longer than two minutes?
Do you intend to study anything that is not maths?
Do you have a wife, husband or both?
Please sing the national anthem when I say the word 'Queen'
And answer the following questions:
why is Britain great?
why everywhere else is not so great?
what is the Anglo Saxon word for great?
do you wear red, white and blue underwear?

Please step this way.
To see if you have answered all these questions truthfully,
we need to do a rectal examination.

322

Remember the number 322.
Three hundred and twenty two.
That's the number of the MPs
who voted against guaranteeing EU citizens
the right to stay in the UK.
322.
Three hundred and twenty two
elected representatives have said to their neighbours,
'if they come for you in the morning
I am one of those who has given all the power
needed for them to take you away.'
You won't need to have done anything wrong,
you won't need to have broken any law.
All you need to be is 'European' .
That's what 322 MPs think is wrong with you.
That's what 322 reasonable, rational MPs have done.
If they come for us in the morning
remember the 322.
Three hundred and twenty two.

Migrant Poetry

Poetry is the migrant: it travels.
Poetry is the witness: it notices.
Poetry is the survivor: it lasts.

Poetry is for Everyone

In private or for sharing, we look at poetry to see if we can find ourselves in it.

The poet suggests. We interpret. That's freedom.

Poetry makes the familiar unfamiliar. And the unfamiliar familiar.

Poetry can tell stories but it doesn't have to. It can talk about the moment. Or the thing.

Poetry can say I Am. Poetry can say We Are.

Poetry can say I Believe. Poetry can say We Believe.

Poetry can stick up for the weak. Poetry can mock the mighty.

Poetry can glorify our rulers or it can dissect them. You choose.

Poetry can dream. It can analyse. It can do both at the same time.

Poetry can say things through its sounds without telling you that this is what it's doing.

Poetry can celebrate. Poetry can mourn. We choose who to celebrate who to mourn.

Poetry begs borrows and steals from all other uses of language and recycles it as poems.

Poetry can change the usual patterns of language.

One way to write poems is to talk with your pen.

Some poems can say things about feelings even though it's only talking about things we can see.

In rhythmic poems the rhythm is made by the 'foot'. In free verse, the rhythm is usually the line.

When children say how do you start to write a poem? I say 'by daydreaming'.

A lot of poems start in a poet's mind with a query.

Beware when the poet says 'I'. It is not the poet. The 'I' is made of words the poet has chosen. The poet is a person.

Most poems repeat something: words, sounds, images, rhythms, meanings. Even opposites are a kind of repetition.

For poets there are no such thing as wow words. For poets all words are wow words. Especially 'the' and 'a'.

Some poems can be mimed.

Poets often walk about looking for ways to begin poems.

Try bringing together two things that don't belong together.

Poems like psychic reality. It's where the feelings are believable even if it's demons or giants or...

There are no right and wrong answers on what poems mean but it does no harm to read or listen to what others say.

Some poems cheat time: they freeze the moment. But they can't cheat the reader's time.

Studying poetry shouldn't be a humiliation.

In science the truth has to be proven. In poetry the truth can be suggested.

If you don't know what a poem means, ask yourself and the person nearest you what it reminds you of. Then ask why or how.

A poem is a poem if the writer and the reader agree it's a poem. If they don't agree, it's under discussion.

Every time you say that something is like another you get a new angle on those two things. Poems often do that.

Many poems don't solve anything. They may start conversations that help you though.

Poets don't know all the meanings of their poems. All the meanings of the poems are made by the poet and the readers.

Poems aren't made of words. They're made of sequences of words.

Poems can capture simultaneous opposites and contradictions when the sound runs counter to the most customary meaning of the words

Think of political poems as if they are political speeches. Only if they are dull, do they not work. Not because they are political.

'Dulce et Decorum est' by Wilfred Owen must be a perfect poem because no Prime Minister so far has recited it at a war memorial. So far.

Brian

A man called Brian came to stay in our flat.
He put all his things in the little room by the front door.

My brother's name is Brian too.
So we have to know who we're talking about
when we say 'Brian'.
We say, 'Big Brian' and 'Little Brian'.

Little Brian knows a lot.
He knows a lot about trains, buses,
planes, bikes, radios, words and jokes.
Big Brian knows even more.
He knows about the whole world.

While we're having breakfast,
I ask a question about something,
like, 'where do clouds go?'
Big Brian says, 'That's a very interesting question.'

Then we go to his room.
In his room there's a mantelpiece over the fire.
On the mantelpiece is the *Encyclopedia Britannica*.

This is a row of books that all look the same
but each one tells you something different about
the whole world.

Big Brian says, 'let's look up "Clouds",
in *Encyclopedia Britannica*.'

He reads the page about 'Clouds'.
He points to a bit that I should read about 'Clouds'.
This is all taking a long time to answer my question
about clouds.

Then we go back to the kitchen.

For my birthday,
Big Brian bought me my favourite, favourite, favourite book.
It's about the naughtiest person who has ever, ever, ever lived.
I love reading about his tricks.
I love saying his name: Til Eulenspiegel,
which you say, 'Till Oylen Shpeegle'.

One day a lady came over.
She wasn't very happy.
Big Brian and her went for a walk.
Big Brian came back on his own.

Sometime after that,
Big Brian packed everything up,
he put his *Encyclopedia Britannica* in a box,
and he left.

Mum and Dad gave me and my brother
the *Oxford Junior Encyclopedia*.
If I ask a question, like 'where does the rain go?'
My brother says,
'That's a very interesting question'
and he finds the page that says 'Rain'
and he points to the bit that I should read about
rain.

I still have my book about Til Eulenspiegel.
Inside the front cover it says,
'Love from Big Brian'.

At 16 My Son Left School

for Joe

At 16 my son left school.
On the day after the last day
I said, 'So how was it?'
He said, 'It was OK, but it wasn't funny.'
'Don't you mean it wasn't 'fun'?' I said.
'No,' he said, 'I mean it wasn't funny.'
'Funny?' I said, 'it wasn't supposed to be funny.
Teachers aren't comedians.'
'Look,' he said, 'before I went to school,
there were loads of jokes. Loads of things
were funny. Then I went to school and
it wasn't funny. Then for years and years
there was school and I kept waiting for it
get funny and it never did. In the
end I realised that it wasn't ever going to
get funny and it didn't. It didn't ever get
funny.'

At 16 my son left school.

Alice under the Floorboards

Under the floorboards of a room at Christchurch College, Oxford, an electrician has found a manuscript thought to have been written by 'Lewis Carroll' (Charles Lutwidge Dodgson). Some of it is hard to decipher and it is clearly incomplete...

I

'Come in,' said a woman in a loud voice.

Alice walked in to a large room at the Compartment of Edification. Sitting in front of her, staring into the middle distance was the Blue Queen.

'How old are you?' said the Blue Queen.
'I'm seven years old,' said Alice politely.

Sitting next to the Queen was the Gibblet.
'Seven?' said the Gibblet, 'Seven? Test her.'
'Test her,' said the Blue Queen.
'Test me?' said Alice, 'but we've only just met.'
'And be robust,' said the Gibblet.
'And be robust,' said the Blue Queen.

Alice heard a scratching sound.
She looked round and observed a row of scribes scratching the word 'robust' on their scrolls.
'Why are you doing that?' enquired Alice.
'To tell the world the good news about robust tests,' they chorused.
'But how do you know "robust Tests" is good news?' asked Alice politely.
'Because the Blue Queen said it is,' chorused the scribes.
'Just because someone says something is something, doesn't mean that it is the thing they say it is,' said Alice.

'Test her!' shouted the Gibblet.
Test her!' shouted the Blue Queen.
'Robustly,' said the Gibblet.
'Robustly,' said the Blue Queen.

'Why do you keep repeating what he says?' said Alice.
'How else would I know what to say?' said the Blue Queen.
'You could think for yourself,' said Alice.
'No, no, no!' screamed the Gibblet. 'That's why we have the tests.'
'What? To help people think for themselves?'
'No, the opposite, you little ninny,' screamed the Gibblet.

'I like opposites,' said Alice. 'I like thinking of things that don't have opposites, like a cupboard, or a coal scuttle.'

'You go on like that, you'll fail the test,' laughed the Gibblet.

'You go on like that, you'll fail the test,' laughed the Blue Queen.

'As far as I'm concerned you've both failed,' said Alice. She turned round and walked out.

II

Alice came to an old stone building.
She walked in and saw some people sitting round a table.
On the table were books and papers, and the people had put rings round some of the words.

One of the people, a friendly-looking Wombat pointed at one of the words and said, 'it's a subjestive!'
Some of the people in the room clapped.
A Frog, just as friendly, looked at it and said, 'it's not a subjestive.'
All the others who hadn't clapped before, clapped now.

Alice came over and looked very hard at the word.
'What do subjestives do?' she asked.
'They subject,' said the Wombat.
'Is it subjesting now?' Alice asked.
'Yes,' said the Wombat.
'No,' said the Frog.

Just then the Gibblet walked in.
Everyone went very quiet.
'Have you done it?' the Gibblet said in a very disagreeable way.
'Yes, we have,' said the Wombat, 'it's all done except for the last one: the subjestive, so because it's not done and we can't agree on it, we would recommend, sir, that we leave it out of the Spadge.'

Alice felt her head going round: first it was the subjestive, now it was the Spadge.

'It will not be left out of the Spadge!' shouted the Gibblet, his giblets shaking with rage.
'But sir...' said the Wombat, 'we cannot ask children to find a subjestive when some of us don't think it's there.'
'Oh yes we can,' said the Gibblet, 'it'll be there if I say it's there.'

'Oooh,' said Alice excitedly. 'Sometimes I say my Boojum is there. And then it's there.'

'That is nothing like subjestives, girl,' said the Gibblet, 'I'm beginning to find you very, very annoying.'

'Oh,' said Alice, 'what are subjestives like then?'

The Gibblet went red.

It all went quiet. The Gibblet got out a little leaflet which was called 'The Spadge'. The Gibblet studied it, turning it over and over.

After a silence that seemed to Alice to be much too long, the Gibblet said, 'Subjestives are things that you find in the Spadge when it says, 'Here are four sentences. Underline the sentence that has the subjestive.''

Alice got excited again. 'Oh I love those, because when you don't know the answer, all you have to do is guess one of them, and one time out of four you'll be right!'

The Gibblet stood up. 'You will not repeat what you have just said anywhere ever, ever, ever!' he said sternly.

'Don't worry,' said Alice, 'I don't need to. We all do that choosing-any-one-of-the-four trick every time we play parlour games. Everyone does.'

'Do they?' said the Gibblet in a shocked voice.

'Well not everyone, actually,' said Alice. 'It's just a trick that some people know. People who don't know end up not choosing any. Then they'll never find the subjestive, will they? So they'll be wrong. It's a shame really. Quite often when I do it, I end up with the right answer.'

'But – but –' spluttered the Gibblet, 'you might not know which one really is the subjestive.'

'And clearly, you don't either,' laughed Alice.

'And while we're doing "and",' said the Frog, 'can I ask why the subjestive is in the Spadge when we haven't finished advising you on what should be in the Spadge ?'

'You people make me sick,' shouted the Gibblet. 'Borogove was right.
You are the Blob. You are all the Blob.'
And he stormed out.

Alice looked at them all.
'Are you the Blob?' she asked, looking for something blobby.
'It's like your Boojum, ' said the Frog, 'if the Gibblet and the Borogove
say the Blob is there, it is there.'

III

The Blue Queen was sitting with her scribes.
Alice sat watching them.

'Today,' said the Blue Queen, 'I'm telling you how it works.'
'Oh good,' said the First Scribe.
'Oh good,' said the Second Scribe.
'Oh good,' said the Third Scribe.
'I know what you're going to say,' said Alice to the Fourth Scribe.
'Oh good,' said the Fourth Scribe.

'How does it work?' said the Queen to the Gibblet.
'You're going to convert all the black and white chess sets into brown and yellow chess sets,' hissed the Gibblet.
'Why?' whispered the Queen back to the Gibblet.
'So that they'll play chess better,' said the Gibblet.
'Will they?' said the Queen.
'Not necessarily,' said the Gibblet.
'So why are we doing it?' asked the Queen.
'Because we hate the black and white chess sets,' said the Gibblet furiously.

Alice heard all this and wondered what the Scribes would make of it.

'Now,' said the Blue Queen to the Scribes, 'we're going to convert all the black and white chess sets into brown and yellow chess sets.'
'Hurrah,' said the Scribes, 'this will make chess better. Hurrah, hurrah, hurrah.'
'Not necessarily,' said Alice.
'Is what that girl said true?' said the Scribes to the Blue Queen.
'Say "We're making chess better!",' whispered the Gibblet to the Queen.
'We're making chess better,' said the Blue Queen.
'But will turning the black and white sets into brown and white sets make chess better?' said Alice.
'We're making chess better,' said the Blue Queen staring into the far distance.
Alice suddenly realised something: something can look like an answer, sound like an answer but not actually be an answer.

'The Blue Queen is making chess better,' chorused the Scribes. Alice picked up a very large stick and...

[*here the manuscript is indecipherable*]

IV

As Alice walked along she could hear the sound of soldiers being drilled. At least, that's what she thought it was.

She came round a corner and saw something that looked to her like an octopus marching to and fro.

The Gibblet was calling out the orders, while the Blue Queen looked on with a fixed stare into the middle distance
'Standards RAISE!' shouted the Gibblet.
The octopus raised its standards, two large flags on which were written 'Standards'.
'Not YOURS!' shouted the Gibblet, 'The Rabble's. Raise the Rabble's standards!'
The octopus now ran towards the Rabble. Alice could see that the Rabble was made up of groups of people – children and grown-ups reading books together.

The octopus was on to them in a flash, snatching the books off them with four or five of its tentacles and handing them brightly coloured little booklets with its other tentacles.

Alice walked over to the Blue Queen.
The Blue Queen nodded at her and said, 'That's my elite squid. 1500.'
'1500?' said Alice, 'But there's only one.'
'1500,' said the Queen.
'It's got 8 legs,' said Alice.
'1500,' said the Queen.

The Gibblet came slithering up.
'And you see what the Rabble have got now?' he said to Alice.
'Brightly coloured booklets?' Alice asked.
'Yes,' said the Gibblet, 'brighty coloured booklets full of dry gaffes.'
'Dry gaffes?' said Alice.
'Yes,' said the Gibblet, 'how else can you read, if you don't learn your dry gaffes?'
'Oh,' said Alice, 'I learned to read without learning my dry gaffes.'

'Then you didn't learn to read PROPERLY,' said the Gibblet.
'Did you learn your dry gaffes?' said Alice.
'No,' said the Gibblet.

'So you didn't learn to read PROPERLY, either,' said Alice to the Gibblet.
The Gibblet hissed loudly.

Alice turned to the Blue Queen.
'What are dry gaffes?' Alice asked her.
The Blue Queen looked into the middle distance and said, 'Dry gaffes are gaffes that are dry.'
'Did you learn your dry gaffes?' Alice asked her.
'The elite squid will raise standards,' the Blue Queen replied.
At which, the squid once again raised the flags marked 'STANDARDS'.
'Not YOURS!!!' screamed the Gibblet, tearing at his giblets in rage.

Alice walked on.

V

As Alice walked along, she was delighted to see that on one side of the road there was a beautiful old building with the word 'Library' on it. Oh, that's just what I need right now, she thought. After all these awful conversations, she was beginning to feel tired and irritated. I could just go inside, sit down on a comfortable chair and read a book.

But just as she walked up the steps to the Library, a frightening creature with big jaws and claws and a giant pair of scissors in his hands, jumped out from behind one of the pillars and roared:

'You can't come in. I have locked the doors. This library is closed.'

'Oh,' said Alice, 'that's a pity. Are you saying that the library is closed for now, or forever?'

'For forever,' said the frightening creature.

'Do you have a name?' said Alice, who had learned that when people say that you can't have something it's always a good idea to find out who they are.

'I am the Georgerwock,' it said, 'don't you know the poem? "Beware the Georgerwock, my son! The jaws that bite, the claws that catch, the scissors that cut, snip, snip, snip!"'

Alice thought for a moment. Yes, she did remember a poem that went something like that but something was different...

'Well, Georgerwock, I think it's a great shame the library is closed. I wanted to read a book. Did you close the library?'

'I did,' said the Georgerwock, 'we have to live within our means.'

'What does that mean?' said Alice.

'It means we can't spend more money than we have,' said the Georgerwock.

'That seems very sensible,' said Alice, 'but a shame all the same I can't read a book.'

The Georgerwock was just about to say something when they both heard a clinking sound. It came from a building next door to the library. Alice looked across to it. It had a big sign outside saying, 'The Counting House.'

'What's that?' said Alice.

'No need to worry your little head about that,' said the Georgerwock.

'Oh I'll look for myself, then,' said Alice and she walked over to the Counting House with the Georgerwock flapping along behind her.

Inside was the King and he was counting out his money.

I'm sure I've heard about that before, thought Alice.

Alice looked through the window at the pile of money sitting on the table in front of the King. It was enormous. And there were sacks more of it sitting behind him and piles on the floor too.

'Are you going to spend all that?' said Alice through the window.

'Good Lord, no,' said the King.

Alice turned to the Georgerwock, 'So why can't we use some of that money to open the library?'

The Georgerwock and the King looked at each other and laughed and laughed and laughed and laughed.

'What I mean,' said Alice to the Georgerwock, 'is when you said "we", "we" had to live within our means, did you count the King in with that "we". Is he part of "we"?'

Again the two of them laughed and laughed and laughed.

'Of course not,' said the Georgerwock, wiping tears of laughter from his face.

'Now you run along, little girl' said the King, 'and don't...'

'...bother my little head about such things?' said Alice in a mocking sort of a way.

'Exactly,' said the Georgerwock.

But Alice thought she would like to find out more about all this.

VI

Alice found herself at a party.
She noticed that the Blue Queen was there, so was the Gibblet, and the Borogove. And a host of others.

A large creature came up to her, mumbling in Latin:
'Ego Loris sum,' he said nodding and trying ineffectually to brush the hair out of his eyes.
'What does that mean?' said Alice.
'It means, "I am Loris"', he said proudly as if that proved something in itself.
'What's going on?' Alice asked.
'This, my girl, this,' barked Loris in a way that suggested that hearing his own voice gave him immense pleasure, 'is the Glory Party. Dulce et decorum est, pro patria mori. And don't you forget it, my girl.'
The moment Loris said this there was a ripple of applause round the whole party.
Alice heard people saying, 'Immense', 'huge', 'marvellous', 'extraordinary', 'genius', 'what a leader' and so on.

Another man came over to her.
'I am Several Chaps,' he said.
'Oh you look like just one,' Alice said.
'I am more than I look,' he said.
'Actually you're less than you look,' said the Blue King and Alice watched while Several Chaps was taken out and put in the bin.

Alice heard someone say:

Bye-bye Grant Shapps
You were Several Chaps.
But it came at price:
none of them was nice.

Mysteriouser and mysteriouser, thought Alice.

A group in the party were huddled round a magic lantern show laughing and slapping their sides.

'Look at this. The Neighbour Party next door are full of Splits.'

Alice looked.

It was indeed.

'They don't know what to do,' the group laughed.

'Now come along', said the Blue King, 'we've got a war to fight.'

It all went quiet.

'What's the matter?' said the Blue King, 'don't tell me that our Glory Party is full of Heeby-jeebies? If it is, I'm going to have to get the Neighbour Party to come and help.'

'Ah hah hah hah,' said all the people in the party, 'the Neighbour Party is full of Splits.'

The Chorus of scribes were there and when they heard about the Neighbour Party's Splits they started writing that down over and over and over again.

'Aren't you interested in the Heeby-jeebies?' Alice asked. 'The Blue King can't go to war if the Glory Party are full of Heeby-jeebies.'

But the Chorus of scribes went on writing, the Neighbour Party is full of Splits. The Neighbour Party is full of Splits. The Neighbour Party is full of Splits... over and over and over again...

Alice walked on.

VII

Alice heard some singing and chanting. She turned to the Blue Queen and said that she wanted to find out more about it.

'Excellent,' said the Gibblet, 'excellent'.

The Blue Queen took Alice to a darkened room and showed her some magic lantern slides. Alice looked at them with amazement. She saw people standing with their eyes shut, she saw people kneeling. Sometimes it was just men, sometimes it was men and women together.

'That's very interesting,' said Alice, 'and are there people who don't do any of this sort of thing?'

The Blue Queen and the Gibblet went very quiet.

'Are there?' said Alice.

'Children like you,' said the Blue Queen, 'need to prepare for life. That's why we showed you lantern slides of different kinds of people.'

'Yes, I know,' said Alice, 'but are there even more different kinds of people who don't do any of this sort of thing? If I knew about them, wouldn't that help me prepare for life too?'

'Don't answer her,' screamed the Gibblet, 'she doesn't need to know. I'm not even sure it is knowledge, anyway.'

The Gibblet opened a huge book called *The Big Book of Knowledge*.

'No, it's not in here,' he said exultantly, and closed the book very quickly.

'If it's not in the *The Big Book of Knowledge*, it's not knowledge,' he added.

'Who wrote this *The Big Book of Knowledge*? asked Alice.

'The Borogove,' said the Blue Queen, her voice trembling with emotion. She shut her eyes.

'The Borogove, the Borogove,' sang the Gibblet in a high pitched lyrical voice as he kneeled down on the floor.

'Have you got the Borogove on one of these lantern slides?' asked Alice.

'One day... one day...' said the Blue Queen in a mysterious way.

Alice walked on.

VIII

Alice was walking down the street when she came across a lump in a doorway.

She bent down to look closer and saw that it wasn't really a lump, it was a person.

'Are you a person?' said Alice.

'Only in a manner of speaking,' said the man – for it was a man.

'Why are you lying in this doorway?' Alice said.

'Where else do you suggest I go?' the man said.

'Home.' said Alice, 'Why don't you go home?'

'Well, now,' said the man. 'I would most certainly go home right now, if I had one.'

'You haven't got a home?' asked Alice.

'Let me explain,' said the man, 'some people deliberately lose their home so that they can get money from the Blatherment, but they're putting a stop to all that.'

'Is that good?' said Alice.

'That puts things right,' said the man.

'Now what?' said Alice.

'Well,' said the man, 'now I don't have a home and I don't have money. That evens things up nicely. I used to have no money but I had a home and that can't be right, can it?'

'Have you got anything to eat?' said Alice.

'Nope,' said the man, 'you see: that matches too – no home, no money, no food.'

Alice felt in her pocket and she still had some of the cake she found earlier. She hoped it wasn't any of that funny food that made her bigger. Or was it smaller? She was just about to hand some to the man, when he stopped her.

'No, no, no, no,' he said, 'that just encourages me.'

'Encourages you to do what?' said Alice.

'Encourages me to live,' said the man.

'Oh, I see,' said Alice, but then she thought that encouraging someone to live sounded like quite a good idea.

'I'm not sure that what you're saying makes sense,' said Alice.

'Look, the way to make people better off,' said the man, 'is to make them poorer. At the moment, I'm doing the poorer bit and at some time later, I'll be better off. Just you see.'

'How long till then?' said Alice.

'Maybe a couple of years,' said the man.

'Won't you need to eat in that time?' Alice asked, 'and it's getting cold. It's not good for you getting cold.'

Just then the door opened. Alice and the man looked in and they could see now that it was some kind of bank.

Maybe they'll let him go in there, thought Alice, but just then two men came out, talking.

'We've turned the corner,' said one.

'Things are getting better,' said the other.

They closed the door of the bank behind them, locked the door several times and walked on.

Alice sat down next to the man in the doorway.

'You see, it's what I said' he said to her, 'things are getting better. Good news, eh?'

'Yes,' said Alice. 'I mean... er...'

But she couldn't finish what she was saying. She wasn't sure that 'getting better' quite said it all.

She looked at the man.

He was lying down again and he had shut his eyes.

IX

Alice found herself in a room full of tables. She was pleased to see the Mad Hatter, Dormouse and March Hare sitting at one. They had stopped trying to stuff the Dormouse into the teapot. They were sitting in a row chanting something she couldn't quite hear. Or, if she could hear it, she couldn't quite understand it. That was because people at the other tables were chanting too.

At another table, the Playing Cards who had once been painting the roses, were now sitting and chanting; and there was Humpty Dumpty and the Caterpillar at another table...

And over there, at another table, were the Walrus and the Carpenter. They had stopped crying over eating oysters... but wait a minute, thought Alice, where are the Oysters?

They were on another table, all in a row, chanting too.

Alice sensed that the Blue Queen and the Gibblet were coming up behind her. They were beaming.
'What do you think?' said the Blue Queen.
'I don't know what to think,' said Alice, 'what's going on? Why are they all here? Why are they sitting at tables? Is this a cafe?'
'No,' snapped the Gibblet, 'of course it isn't. These are Times Tables.'
'I see,' said Alice, though in truth she didn't.
'Everyone sits at Times Tables now,' said the Blue Queen proudly, checking with the Gibblet that this was the right thing to say.
'This one,' said the Gibblet, pointing at the one with the Walrus and the Carpenter, 'is the top Times Table.'
'And this one,' said the Blue Queen proud as ever, and pointing to the Oysters, 'is the bottom Times Table.'
'We're the bottom Times Table,' echoed the Oysters, 'because we're no good at Times Tables. Listen!'

Alice listened as they chanted: 'once one is one, two ones are two, three ones are three...'

She was puzzled.

'They sound alright to me,' she said.

'Too slow,' said the Gibblet.

'Too slow,' said the Blue Queen.

'How slow is slow?' said Alice.

'This slow,' hissed the Gibblet, showing her a complicated-looking machine he was carrying. He pulled a lever, there was a whirring and clicking and out came a ticket. He handed it to Alice. On the ticket, it said, 'Slow is 12 mph, fast is 3 times as fast as slow, which is 36 mph.'

'Thank you,' said Alice. 'That's a very handy machine.'

'Yes,' said the Gibblet proudly, 'it's my Times Tables machine.'

'I think we can be just as proud of the Walrus and the Carpenter,' said the Blue Queen, 'listen to how they chant.'

And sure enough, they whizzed through their Times Tables faster than the March Hare could run.

'You're very fast,' said Alice, 'if slow is 12 mph and fast is 3 times as fast, do you think you're going that fast?'

'I don't understand you,' said the Walrus, who was beginning to get a bit hungry.

'Well,' said one of the Oysters, 'I think you're 3 times as fast as us, aren't you? We're very, very slow. You're very, very fast. You're much better than us, aren't you?'

'I don't know,' said the Walrus, 'that's not what we're doing today.'

'Exactly!' said the Gibblet who was beginning to get a little worried about the way Alice was asking all these questions.

'I'm hungry,' said the Walrus.

'Me too,' said the Carpenter.

The Blue Queen and the Gibblet took up a position of policemen directing traffic. They pointed towards the slowest Times Table where the Oysters sat.

Alice watched while the Walrus and the Carpenter went over to the Oysters and started to eat them.

The Gibblet and the Blue Queen watched too, nodding and smiling. Alice thought that they were very pleased with the way things were working out.

X

The Blue Queen and the Gibblet wanted to show Alice something.

'This,' said the Blue Queen, 'is a glass-room. It's made of glass so we can see into it. We can see everything that's going on in there.'

'It looks nice,' said Alice, 'what do you do in there?'

'WE don't do anything in the glass-room,' hissed the Gibblet, 'We put children in the glass-room.'

'Why?' said Alice.

'To fill them up with knowledge, of course,' said the Gibblet.

Alice looked in to the glass-room. There were rows and rows of children in there but they didn't seem to be being filled up with knowledge. Alice was puzzled. She remembered from... where was it? Before she fell down the hole, when she went to school, there was a person there they called a 'teacher'. In the glass-room, there was no teacher.

'Excuse me,' said Alice, 'isn't there supposed to be a teacher in the glass-room?'

'There is a teacher in the glass-room,' said the Blue Queen.

'There is a teacher in the glass-room,' said the Gibblet.

Alice stared again. She didn't want to annoy them but she believed in saying true things. So she said, 'Where?'

'The teacher,' said the Blue Queen, 'is where the teacher is.'

'Very good,' said the Gibblet, 'exactly. The teacher is where the teacher is because the teacher couldn't be where the teacher is not.'

'We're not running out, you know,' said the Blue Queen.

'I didn't think you were running anywhere,' said Alice.

'No, no, no,' said the Blue Queen, 'we're not running out of teachers. We've got loads of them.'

'Loads of them,' repeated the Gibblet.

'But not actually here. In this Glass-room,' said Alice.

'We've told you,' said the Blue Queen, 'there is a teacher in the glass-room.'

'And if we've told you something is what it is, then it is!' said the Gibblet.

Alice tried to understand this but she couldn't.

Just then some heralds blew trumpets and called out:

'The Blue King is going to make an announcement! The Blue King is going to make an announcement!'

This made the Scribes very excited and they all wrote down, 'The Blue King is going to make an announcement.'

The Blue King stepped forward and said, 'I have good news. This year there will be no more poor people.'

At this, everyone started clapping and cheering. Even the Scribes stopped writing for a moment to clap and cheer before getting back to the hard work of writing, 'There will be no more poor people.'

'Where will they go?' said Alice.

Everyone went very quiet.

Then the Gibblet said, 'the poor people won't be anywhere, because they can't be anywhere if they're not there.'

The Scribes loved that too and scribbled that down.

Alice looked at her hand. She wondered if by saying it's not there, it would disappear. Or, as she was feeling a bit hungry, if she said that a sandwich was in front of her, it would appear.

She was just about to try when...

[*the manuscript ends here*]

Times Tables

Some can learn tables.
Some can't.
Some can use the tables and understand maths.
Some can't.
You can know the tables and be good at maths.
You can know the tables and be no good at maths.
You cannot know the tables and be no good at maths.
You can be no good at tables and be good at maths.
Knowing the tables is not the be all and end all of maths.
Maths is more than tables.
If you have a high stakes test on tables, you end up saying to
        children that maths is knowing the tables.
You end up saying to them that the most important thing
        about maths is knowing the tables.
Giving them a high stakes test which will judge the child,
        the teacher and the school, will add one more stress to
        education.

Vulgar

When we did our first lesson in vulgar fractions at school
there were children who giggled.
I didn't get the joke.
'Vulgar', they said.
'Why's that funny?' I said.
'Rude', they said.
'What's rude?' I said.
'Vulgar', they said.
I had never met the word 'vulgar'.
In fact, my mother and father
were people who the kind of person
who used the word 'vulgar'
might have called 'vulgar'.
But my mum and dad didn't call it 'vulgar'.

So I didn't get the joke.

Subject Knowledge

Is 'how to sell crap that no one needs' subject knowledge?
Is 'how someone gets and tries to hold power over you' a
    subject knowledge?
Is 'how to spot that someone is deceiving you' a subject
    knowledge?
Are 'how I teach' and 'how I learn' forms of subject
    knowledge?
Who decides which subjects and which parts of subject
    knowledge are the subject knowledge to be taught?
Does the subject 'how to find things out' count as a 'subject
    knowledge'?

The 'Expected Level'

according to the National Curriculum

If you can write and make sense
remember, it's not enough
if you can write and make people laugh
remember, it's not enough
if you can write and make people cry
remember, it's not enough
if you can write and make people desperate to know what
happens next,
remember, it's not enough
if you can write and make people feel good,
remember, it's not enough
if you can write and make people think and wonder,
remember, it's not enough
if you can write and make people want to be where you went,
remember, it's not enough
if you can write and make people want to be some of the people
you've written about
remember, it's not enough
if you can write and make people want to read more and more
and more
remember, it's not enough.

But:
if you can write something
that no one is particularly interested in,
no one is desperate to read more and more,
no one laughed or cried or wanted to be where you went
or wanted to know what happened next,
no one wondered about what you had written,
yet,
you included commas, semi-colons, colons,
expanded noun phrases, fronted adverbials, and
embedded relative clauses
over and over and over again

that's enough.

Success

People don't understand that
the success of British capitalism
depends on whether
5-year olds know
what a split digraph is.

Comprehension

'Billy has a blue hat – what colour is his hat?'
'Blue.'
'Correct. One mark.'

'It is raining – why is he wearing a hat?'
'Cos he supports Chelsea.'
'Wrong – no mark.'

Children Writing

Writing is part of the human conversation.
We have to show children they are entitled to join in.
No passport required.
One of several good ways to learn to write is to compare in
      detail examples of good writing.
We have to stop indicating to children they have nothing to
      say and don't know how to say it.

How to Guarantee Teacher Shortages

Encourage the press to run stories saying that teachers are lazy and that there are thousands of bad ones.

Get the head of Ofsted to say the same.

Keep this up for decades (both main parties).

Bring in hundreds of measuring and assessment systems, levels, targets, tests, exams, which then breed more 'rehearsal' tests and exams.

Bring in a punitive, rapid, unsupportive inspection system which ignores the fact that scores are attached to children so that if you're in a school where there has been turnover the inspectorate say that has nothing to do with us.

Run a new kind of school where the salaries of management are not open to public scrutiny.

Allow interest groups to open schools which take on proportionally fewer SEN, EAL and FSM pupils than nearby LA schools.

Allow covert selection and exclusion processes to take place around these new kinds of schools because the LA schools have to pick up the pieces.

Use international data as if it is holy writ and ignore evidence that suggests that comparing countries does not compare like with like, that some countries which are 'top' are selecting. Obscure the differences between the countries by only talking about 'places' in the table, without ever making clear whether these differences are 'significant' or not.

Use China as an example of utopia in education without making a comparison between the two societies – as if education exists separately from the societies that produce the respective education systems.

Make sure that very nearly all the people running the state education system from government have no, or very little, state education experience themselves.

The PISA Tables

'Quick, look at the PISA tables!
Are we moving up, are we moving down?
The PISA tables tell us everything we need to know.
Are we a good country?
Are we a bad country?
The PISA tables will tell us.
If we're going down, we're a bad country
and that's teachers fault.

A bad country is one which won't compete.
This is teachers' fault.
The fate of British capitalism
rests in teachers' hands.

There are no other factors
in the matter of success or failure of British capitalism.
The only factor is where we are on the PISA tables.

Being very good at education and statistics
teaches me this.

I know all about the PISA tables.
I know all about being competitive.
I know all about British capitalism.

Teachers you are rubbish.

Quick, look at the PISA tables!'

Let's Franchise Schools!

'I am standing as parent governor at Local Street Comprehensive because I want to do all I can to make the school efficient, competitive and 21st Century. I promise to do all I can to get it turned into an Academy and, if you elect me, I will do all I can to develop the assets of the site. Among my many ideas for this are: inviting franchises in to take over the classrooms on the ground floor, turning the gym into a commercially successful fitness and spa, getting rid of the library and turning it into a hi-tech media centre for local aspiring entrepreneurs. I will work with Pearson or any other major company to convert the curriculum to a digital platform and will encourage them to make us an offer we can't refuse to provide us with tablets. We need many more vending machines in the school and these can be used to fund school trips to successful businesses in the area. There are far too many school trips to so-called 'educational' sites. We need to get the students thinking business, business, business.

On the discipline front, I'm proposing that the school bring in one-strike-and-out. One of my interests in the community is that I am running the first commercially viable pupil referral unit in the country, and I am delighted to say that schools all over the area send troublesome and challenging pupils to my unit to experience the tried and proven boot-camp regime. So far, we have successfully released more than 30% of the boys into the armed services, 30% into HM Prisons and very few have committed suicide.

Please vote for me.'

Listen up

Listen up students:
only study what you know will get you a job.
We don't know what will get you a job
but only study what you know will get you a job.

We don't know what will get you a job
for two reasons:
1. We can't read the future.
2. We've got rid of many jobs because we don't think we
    should make things in this country.

This leaves accountancy, banking, insurance
and people who make it all possible:
company lawyers.

Those are jobs.

Listen up students:
only study what you know will get you a job.
We don't know what will get you a job.
What's more
we don't even know if those jobs I mentioned
just now will be jobs
because maybe the firms that have those jobs
will disappear off this island too.

Listen up students
only study what you know will get you a job.

Unemployment Figures

How to make sure
that it looks as if unemployment is going down:

Take two people who want to work 40 hours a week
and give them each a 20-hours-a-week job.

This is one 40 hour job
and one invisible, uncounted unemployed person.

Release a monthly figure telling us that unemployment
is going down.

Rely on the press and TV to say that unemployment
is going down.

Unemployment figures.
Or doesn't figure.

Chairs

Two people are sharing a bit of bread. It's all they've got to eat today. In the corner of the room, someone is eating a huge meal. A politician walks in and says that he's collecting tax. He takes a part of the bit of bread from the two who are sharing bread. He goes over to the person eating the huge meal. He takes a bit from the plate.

The people eating the bread are sitting on the floor. They say, 'Can we have a chair?' The politician says, 'No, times are tough, we can't afford chairs in the present climate.' The people sharing the bread say that the politician took a quarter of their bread but only took a corner of the other person's meal. An argument breaks out about how unfair that is, but the politician explains that that's the law and anyway, last time anyone tried to collect anything off the person eating the huge meal, they didn't get anything.

The politician leaves.

The two people sharing the bread are wondering about the chair. The person eating the big meal is on a chair. One of them remembers from another time that the person eating the big meal has many, many chairs. He remembers seeing the chairs when he was cooking the meal for the person.

The politician comes back into the room and says things are getting better and goes out again.

A Great Global Trading Nation

This 'great global trading nation'
that Theresa May is going on about:
what are we supposed to be trading?
What great array of products are we offering
that the world is queuing up for?
Pork pies? Kendal mint cake?

Perhaps when the royals go for their global joints,
when they go along the lines of adoring people,
they should wear usherettes' trays,
as if they were selling ice creams in the theatre
but instead of ice creams on their trays,
they could carry little bits of Melton Mowbray pork pies,
Kendal mint cake and Eccles cakes.
Just like people stand outside shops in shopping malls,
giving away little cubes of spicy sausage and chocolate.
That would show 'em.
The British economy would suddenly go on a massive uptick
as the world sucked up every bit
of pork pie, mint cake and Eccles cakes
that the factories could produce.

A Strong Economy

'Strong economy'
NHS cuts
'Strong economy'
Cuts in school budgets
'Strong economy'
Wages not keeping up with inflation
'Strong economy
Punitive sanctions system with benefits
'Strong economy'
Rise in zero hour contracts
'Strong economy'
Bogus 'self-employed' contracts so as to avoid workers' rights
'Strong economy'
Unequal pay
'Strong economy'
Bogus apprenticeships.

'Strong economy'
Strong for who?

Buy it, Want it, Need it

Human beings have always had needs. At hominids emerged in evolution, co-operating to hunt and survive, we made tools and hunting weapons in order to do that. That said, when I went to Grimes Graves I was told that Neolithic people also produced flints that were identical as those used for hunting and skinning but hoarded them. So, there are piles of brand new, unused flints in mini-hoards. The reckoning is that they are for some kind of ritual or religious purpose, perhaps as votive offering to the gods thanking him/her/them for enabling the hunt or wishing that the god/goddess would bring it to fruition. Either way, it's a 'surplus' of objects that these people have made – beyond practical needs or use. In other words, early on in societies, humans discovered they could produce stuff beyond utility.

Between then and now, humans also discovered that you can produce objects for play and leisure and that these can be sold. They discovered that even the most basic items of basic, essential need can be sold – the clothes we absolutely need to cover ourselves against the weather, and of course foodstuffs. And then beyond that, even, humans found that we can sell images of ourselves to each other, we can sell ideas, we can sell each other (slavery, prostitution, football players). Even the 'basic-need' products can be turned into items that appear to be more worthy than others based on what they look like rather than what is in their content: a packet of crisps can be more 'desirable' than a bit of protein that I need. We now live in a world where virtually anything and everything, anybody, any feeling is itself marketable, or, just as importantly, can be used, adopted or adapted to make something else marketable.

For all these things to be sold, they have to be produced. You have to have a system (or several interlocking systems) of production. The present system involves bringing people together in order for owners to make profits. That's the only system available today. Now, when politicians talk, they talk as if the function and purpose of production is to bring us all these goods that we consume. So, when they talk about 'the economy' or 'Britain doing better' and the like, and 'living standards' they imply that this is all about the pleasure we get from going beyond subsistence into consuming the things we like and want and desire. What's more, in order to reach this point of pleasure, we have to have the profit-making system. Otherwise we wouldn't have all that pleasure and gratified desire. (Let's leave to one side for the moment, that millions don't get to gratify the desires created by the system because they don't have the means – money – to get what they want!)

So, our consumerism becomes the justification for profit-making. Profits, we should remember, are what's pocketed by owners. The need to make a tiny group of people rich becomes, in their language, the essential and only way in which we can become satisfied. Their wealth is our means to become happy, they are telling us. We must help them become rich. (Of course they don't express it exactly in those terms.)

This puts into context the kinds of 'news' reports we hear which talk about retail sales as a problem for all of us. So, if Tesco's sales, say, are going down, the news report invites us to share in the worry about this. We hear about how this or that is going to 'stimulate' demand. We need to be buying more, they tell us. We need to be buying more so that these firms can 'do better'.

Now, pull back from that. Do we need to be buying more because we need what they are selling us? OK, sometimes. But not all the time. And not all of the stuff they say we need. In fact, they're not bothered whether we need it or not. We just have to have it – not because we actually need it, but in order for the owners to secure the profits they need. We consume for them. Not for us. And yet it 'feels' as if it's for us. 'I'm going to buy another jumper.' Not 'I'm going to buy something that will help the owners of Jumper Inc. become richer.'

Bad People

They love us to have people we think of as 'bad'.
We have to have 'bad people'.
We're supposed to love having bad people.
We wouldn't be able to get by without bad people.
We're supposed to like having bad people in newspaper
headlines.
We're supposed to like having bad people talked about on the
radio.
Bad people make us feel better than them.
We are glad we are good and they are bad.
People come on TV and tell us that they are
going to deal with the bad people.
They are going to stop the bad people.
They list what the bad people do
and it's all bad.
And there are always too many bad people,
And the bad people are doing things that stop us doing good
things.
So the people on the TV have plans for the bad people:
new laws are needed
new places to put the bad people
more people in uniform to make sure the bad people
don't spread.
This talk about bad people
makes us like the people who come on TV
to tell us these things.
We'll feel safer if these TV people are in charge.
C'mon, we say, deal with the bad people now:
do bad things to the bad people
that's the way to show we are good
we have no choice
sometimes we just have to be bad to be good.

C'mon.

Inequality

As Minister for Telling Everyone That Things Are OK Really,
I'd like to repeat that inequality is not really a problem.

Apart from anything else, it's clear that income inequality is coming
down.

This means that we don't take into consideration such things as
tax avoidance, wealth acquired through rent, sale of assets and
dividends from shares which has enabled people to become
extraordinarily wealthy.

But then we don't want people to focus on that sort of thing
because it breeds envy.

In the meantime I'm going to keep going on about
how inequality is coming down, and life is getting better for all.
Thank you.

Integration and Opportunity

The Not-Casey Report looked at how people with wealth avoid contact with the lower classes.

Not-Casey Report on upper classes examined ownership of the media; finding disturbing examples of it repeating same ideas over and over again.

Not-Casey Report on upper classes found disturbing examples of 'marrying in' and 'marrying of their own kind'.

Not-Casey Report on upper classes: Not-Casey on @BBCr4today later to talk about widening inequality means segregation.

Not-Casey Report on upper classes: disturbing examples of tax avoidance/dodging; non-dom expatriation of capital; lobbying of MPs...

The Not-Casey Report on upper classes: entrenched examples of inherited wealth dominating leading positions is business/society.

The Not-Casey Report published later today on segregation of the upper classes: examples of in-breeding/gated living/private education and health. #worrying

The Coronation

In 1953, my father would like to tell the story of the Coronation.
He said that us and the Aprahamians decided to avoid it.
We would go camping. In boats.
They hired punts on the River Thames, loaded on some tents
and with no radios anywhere near us
we would be Coronation-proof.
No sight or sound of the Coronation would reach us.
I remember the paddles and the awning that we had to take
down when the wind blew
and a dangerous moment near Wallingford when we nearly went
over the weir
while my brother said that this holiday was the most
boring holiday we had ever been on.
One day, my father said, he and Francis Aprahamian,
went into Wallingford to do the shopping
and thought they would pop into a pub.
Just as they walked through the door,
they realised that the place was packed:
they were all watching a television.
The bloke whose job it is to put the crown on the queen's head
was standing hovering over her, with the crown in his hands.
As Francis and my dad pushed open the door,
everyone in the pub turned angrily towards Francis and my Dad
with a giant 'shhhhhhhhhhhhhh!'
and then they turned back to the moment they had all been
waiting for.
When my father told the story,
the shushing obviously bugged him
but the bit that really irritated him
was that in the one split second
as him and Francis pushed open the door
he did actually see the crown being
lowered on the queen's head.

Royal News

I don't mind waiting
I do mind being told I'm waiting
I don't mind good news
I do mind being told which news is good
I don't mind being told that people are happy
I do mind being told that I'm happy
I don't mind that people like a newborn baby
I do mind being told that I like a newborn baby
I don't mind that people like doing their family tree
I do mind being told that I like their family tree
I don't mind being rained over
I do mind being reigned over.

We All Need Doctors

'We all need doctors. The thing is, what we don't need are Junior Doctors. Doctors are brilliant, hard-working, brave, overworked people who save lives. Junior Doctors are greedy, deluded and destructive people, who have let themselves become controlled by a small group of Trotskyites who jeopardise the security of the country. I love Doctors. I once went to see a Doctor. So did my wife. And my children. They made us better. That's the kind of work that Doctors do. I once saw a Junior Doctor in a car park outside a hospital. Why wasn't she in the hospital? That's what you get with Junior Doctors. One moment they're in the hospital, the next they're in the Car Park. Small wonder we need to close Accident and Emergency departments. I think we need the NHS 24/7. The Junior Doctors don't. They would rather be in the Car Park. I've always loved and admired doctors. My wife too. I've got a bad foot.'

The Jeremy Hunt Book of Wisdom

'*We may well need more doctors and nurses. But if you're worried about a rash your child has, an online alternative – where you look at photographs and say 'my child's rash looks like this one' – may be a quicker way of getting to the bottom of whether this is serious or not.*'
Jeremy Hunt

I would like to be Jeremy Hunt's speech writer and offer him the following suggestions as press releases:

Jeremy Hunt says that people should improve their bandaging skills by watching *The Curse of the Mummy's Tomb.*

Jeremy Hunt says using Google for self-diagnosis is good for you, good for the NHS, good for Google and what's good for Google is good for us all.

Jeremy Hunt say that a heart attack is sometimes best cured by wiggling your fingers.

Jeremy Hunt says that brain tumours are often alleviated by eating prunes.

Jeremy Hunt says that many illnesses can be cured with a nice cup of tea.

Jeremy Hunt says that a fever can often be brought down by having a sympathetic chat with someone.

Jeremy Hunt says that broken bones are often best cured with a good rest. Just put your feet up. If you can, that is.

Jeremy Hunt says that doctors waste too much time trying to find out if people are ill.

Jeremy Hunt says he isn't ill, so why should anyone else be?

Jeremy Hunt says that epidemics are a luxury. People should just sit a bit further away from each other.

Jeremy Hunt says that too much time is taken up in the NHS by people who are ill.

Jeremy Hunt says that eating your own underwear is a proven cure for the plague.

Jeremy Hunt says that careful use of a mirror can enable you to take your own appendix out.

Jeremy Hunt says that a good deal of dietary complaints could be solved by us eating each other.

Jeremy Hunt says that illness is something caused by doctors.

Jeremy Hunt says that we don't need Junior Doctors. We need Senior Doctors.

Jeremy Hunt says that if you cover one eye up and then swap to the other eye, it cures pneumonia.

Jeremy Hunt says that his ambition in life is to have a rash named after him.

Jeremy Hunt says that when a vet sees a sick cow, the cow doesn't write to her MP complaining about the vet service.

Jeremy Hunt says that people should dig their own graves.

Jeremy Hunt says that people can choose not to be ill.

Jeremy Hunt says if you've got a bad leg, when you go to work, leave it at home.

Jeremy Hunt says that doctors' surgeries are much too full of people who are ill.

Jeremy Hunt says, if the GPs want to resign, let them. 'I'll do their job.'

Jeremy Hunt says I know all about medicine, I was born in a hospital.

Jeremy Hunt says that when he was at Junior School he wasn't paid, so why should Junior Doctors be.

Jeremy Hunt says no one likes doctors in surgeries, so he's closing surgeries, putting doctors in cabs, and patients will now roam the streets looking for a doctor-cab.

Jeremy Hunt says GPs need to spend more of their time and budgets on marketing themselves. Doctors should think of themselves as coca-cola cans.

Jeremy Hunt says that he knows of a doctor who died. That's why we can't always rely on there being a doctor when we need one.

Jeremy Hunt says Tories laughing at sick people in Corbyn's letters is good. If more people laughed, there'd be less strain on the NHS.

Jeremy Hunt says that if he inserts his head into his anus he finds the view much more interesting than when thinking about the NHS.

Jeremy Hunt's contract says he doesn't have to work at weekends.

Jeremy Hunt says everyone knows he'll be running the NHS long after all the Junior Doctors have become hedge fund managers and estate agents

Jeremy Hunt says he doesn't want to be guilty of misrepresentation but he would just like to point out Junior Doctors are mass murderers.

Jeremy Hunt says making a contract doesn't have to be between two parties. He likes doing it with himself.

Jeremy Hunt says he's had another look at the stats and discovered that no one dies between Monday and Friday.

Jeremy Hunt says that lots of poor people aren't safe where they live so why should they have safety if they are patients in hospital?

Jeremy Hunt says that when Britain was great, barbers were surgeons, so he's asking barbers and hairdressers to be doctors.

Jeremy Hunt says the NHS was a socialist plot to undermine Winston Churchill.

Jeremy Hunt says this cradle to the grave malarkey is a bit sentimental. He says he's not in a cradle or a grave and he's getting along fine.

Jeremy Hunt says the Junior Doctors are unpopular because no sick person really wants a doctor to help make them better.

Jeremy Hunt says at least Hitler made the doctors run on time.

Jeremy Hunt says what is all this childish attachment to a National Health Service? Why not a Branson Health Service? Or a Murdoch one?

Jeremy Hunt says why in heaven's name would doctors know anything about the health service?

Jeremy Hunt says too many doctors behave as if they have a mind of their own.

Jeremy Hunt says any Junior Doctor breaking his contract will be dismissed and if that means sacking all of them so much the better.

Jeremy Hunt says he was born to lead and Junior Doctors were born to follow.

Jeremy Hunt says Junior Doctors are like dogs and can and must be brought to heel.

Jeremy Hunt says doctors are the middle man between life and death and he's just trying to cut out the middle man.

Jeremy Hunt says if you have a pint of water in 5 bottles, then put the pint into 7 bottles, the pint becomes more than a pint.

Jeremy Hunt says if the Junior Doctors don't accept the deal he'll get unemployed school leavers do their job.

Jeremy Hunt says that he's been talking to some dead people who've told him that the Junior Doctors should get back to work.

Jeremy Hunt says the way to get more and better beer is tip your pint into several glasses.

Jeremy Hunt says Junior Doctors should stop walking between hospital wards and run instead.

Jeremy Hunt says if you take some butter you were going to put on one slice and spread it across two slices you get more butter.

Jeremy Hunt says all the NHS chiefs support me apart from the ones who don't.

Jeremy Hunt says Junior Doctors travelling to work by rail should drive the train.

Jeremy Hunt says, On Friday night hospitals lock their doors and people die on the doorsteps till the staff come back in on Monday morning.

Jeremy Hunt's contract says he doesn't have to work at weekends.

Jeremy Hunt says everyone knows he'll be running the NHS long after all the Junior Doctors have become hedge fund managers and estate agents.

What Can You Do?

They know that obesity shortens life expectancy,
they know that certain cheap foods have incredibly high
        calorie count,
they know that these foods are produced, distributed
and sold by paying people incredibly low wages,
but, hey, there's nothing a society can do about it...

Carry on.

Leader-talk

O am I so tired of leader-talk
suddenly we all need a leader.
People who get bossed about
by owners of newspapers
tell us we need a leader,
they do leader recipes
what makes a good leader.
What makes a good leader
they say
is someone who we all realise
is our leader.
That's a leader.
Then, after they've been leader
they write books about
the rise and fall of the leader.
They say the leader had a fatal flaw.
The fatal flaw is that they thought
they could be the leader.
Never mind.
We all need a leader.
Sometimes it's important,
(they say) that the leader doesn't tell the whole truth.
We're not ready for the whole truth.
Only the leader and his friends
are ready for the whole truth.
What is 'not the whole truth'?
Not the whole truth is lies.
The leader must tell lies.
We love the leader
then we love the lies.
And we love charisma.
If someone says that they want to take a picture of you,
then tell them that you're going to shut your eyes
and when you open them
that's the exact moment they have to take the photo.

That's charisma. Right there.
That's how important charisma is.
When you're talking
try to say everything is three.
Say things like:
blah blah blah
or I want people to have blah
I want people to have blooh
I want people to have bleeh.
Three is charisma too.
The people being bossed about
by the people who own newspapers and TV channels
will say you were convincing,
if you've got charisma.
The idea here is:
them saying that the leader is convincing
makes them sound convincing.
It's a convincing machine.
We come out the end of the machine
convinced
and we will say we need a leader
we need a leader
we need a leader
(see, I did that three times).

Corbyn Wins the Leadership Vote

I loved
that moment when the commentator
said that Jeremy Corbyn had won the contest
'in spite of' his radical politics.
And there was me thinking that Jeremy
Corbyn won the contest
'because of' his politics.

Thank you media.
Got another message this morning:
we can't have socialism through action
outside of parliament
because parliament is the will of the people;

and we can't have socialism
through parliament
because no one in parliament wants socialism.

Sorted.

Corbyn and the Cauliflower Man

On the night that Jeremy Corbyn won,
over on the World TV News Channel,
following a harrowing look at the destruction in Syria
they showed a journalist asking Jeremy Corbyn
where he got his jumper from.

All over the world, within a few seconds,
we viewers could flip from
thinking of whole cities in Syria
lying devastated to: Jeremy's jumper,
and I wondered if any journalist has ever put a
microphone under David Cameron's nose
and said

'So, Mr Cameron, do you think you can
renegotiate the terms for Britain's membership
of the EU and where did you get your shirt?'

Following the jumper revelations,
in a matter of seconds,
this world news package wanted to give us
an insight into how people have reacted to
Jeremy Corbyn's victory
and once again they went to see the
all-in-one, standby, representative British voter:

the bloke in the market selling cauliflowers.

Why is it always him?
Spare him a moment's sympathy:
around every election time
thousands of journalists scour the country
trying to put their finger on the pulse
trying to gauge which way the wind is blowing
and they all end up at his market stall.

He's just trying to sell cauliflowers.

That's his job.

He goes to a wholesale depot at 4 in the
morning and buys
the cauliflowers that are just on the turn
and puts them on his stall.

He's tired, he's cold,
can't you journalists leave him alone?
he's just trying to get rid of 50 cauliflowers
and you're asking him
what he thinks of Jeremy Corbyn?

Who knows –
possibly the only thing he remembers
about Jeremy Corbyn –
thanks to you guys –
is:

Jeremy Corbyn's got a jumper.

For Jeremy Corbyn

Fresh from:

proclaiming the virtues of the
1000 year dynasty, the British monarchy;

advising us of the special qualities of a
non-elected second chamber
with its origins in Norman rule;

celebrating an economic system
that was developed and finessed
with the use of child labour around 1810;

continuing to solve international disputes
with the 10,000 year old method of
killing those you disagree with;

they tell us that socialism is outdated.

How Corbyn Lost Oldham

Corbyn became Leader of the Labour Party. There was a by-election in Oldham. The papers predicted Labour would lose. Labour won the by-election.

'I am very grateful to this newspaper for giving me an opportunity to respond to the Oldham by-election – and indeed to respond to every aspect of Corbynism since it first appeared.

I was one of the first to notice Corbyn's jumper as a key part of why he would fail to win the Labour leadership contest and though I wasn't entirely right in that matter, I think I can say with confidence that he would have won Oldham by more votes had he worn a suit and tie.

Again, I spotted the fact that Corbyn has spent a lifetime on the backbenches. I don't think anyone had noticed that before, so I made that public.

More importantly, I've been able to write and talk about that again and again. And again and again... and how Corbyn has split the Labour Party. The Labour Party used to be united. All the time. In the Blair era, the Labour Party had a great, charismatic leader who united the party round the need to kill people in the Middle East. This was a major achievement and everyone in the press – and therefore the world – are in great admiration of him for doing that.

The moment Corbyn came in, he gave support to the little ragbag of outsiders, losers, has-beens and wannabees, while the people who could really unite the party have been pushed to the edges. That's why I am so glad that the TV companies give these great unity-creators such a good

airing day in day out, to come on to the TV
and explain how bad Corbyn is. This unites the party.
Obviously.

Now to Oldham: well not literally. I've never been there.
Oldham was a disaster for Corbyn.
If he hadn't been the leader, Oldham would
have been a 100% Labour-voting constituency.
No one would have voted Tory, UKIP or LibDem.
As it was, thousands of people refused to vote for Corbyn.

Even so, there is clearly something wrong with the people
of Oldham because some of them did actually vote Labour.

I look forward to being on *Question Time, Any Questions,
Sky News, ITV News, Channel 4 News*, Channel Five,
Five Live, World at One, the Daily Politics, to put
these crucial ideas across.

I'm not actually an MP any more but I do have a place
in the House of Lords though I haven't been able to get
there recently as I am spending more time with my
yachts.'

Threat

One of the most deadly, terrifying things ever to have happened
to anyone ever,
is the sight of gangs of screaming, murderous,
dervish-like Corbyn-supporters, demanding
that people like me should stop supporting the bombing of Syria.

Let's get this straight,
bombing Syria is good, wholesome, clean and kind.
Of course people will be killed.
These will be ISIS-IS-ISL-Daesh people or Daesh-ISL-ISIS-IS
people
or IS-Daesh or ISL-ISIS who we have
identified.
They are easy to identify. They are fascists.
Fascists like the ones in Spain in 1936.
Or Nazis in Germany in 1933.
Or in Italy in... er... then.
Or in Chile with Pinochet.
That's what ISL-IS-Dash are.
Just the same. No difference.
We British got rid of them.
Well, OK, not in Spain but that's different.
And not Pinochet either, actually.
But that's different too and I don't want to go into that just now.
Please don't interrupt.
And OK we didn't get rid of the Nazis entirely on our own.
Some others helped us.
A bit.
Not very much.

Anyway, we were freedom fighters then
fighting for the freedom of the British Empire
which was entirely free for everyone in
the British Empire – Africa, India, West Indies,
all free.
And we defended that.

We fought for freedom in Iraq
when we were threatened by Weapons of Mass Destruction.
Are there any Weapons of Mass Destruction there now?
No.
Exactly.
And there are a lot fewer people there.
That's thanks to us too.

And that's the kind of thing we're defending now.

Apart from Corbyn and his terrorist supporters.
When we kill with our planes
that is good, kind killing because
the only people that will be killed
will be the Nazi-Daesh-ISL-Franco-ISIS thing,
unlike the foul, despicable terrorism of Corbyn's supporters
which is jeopardising the very heartbeat of democracy.

We will not waver.
We are valiant for truth.'

Unknown MP Resigns from Obscure Committee

'You won't know me, but I am a member of a parliamentary Labour sub-committee that you've never heard of and it gives me enormous pain to say that I'm going to have to resign. I'm afraid, here I am on television and if there's one thing I really didn't want to do, it's come on television. I'm hating being on television. I really am. Later, "The Westminster Bubble" show is going to be covering this, which I think is an excellent thing because this matter of me being unknown and a member of a committee you haven't heard of, really needs to be aired. It's a major news item and shows just how deeply divided the Corbynistas have made our beloved Labour Party. In fact, the people who run the "The Westminster Bubble" are good honest people who have no vested in interest in saying that the Labour Party is deeply divided and the group I belong to – called "Suspect" – have no vested interest or ulterior motive in talking about a divided Labour Party. The whole thing makes me very sad. Could I just say hello to my mother?'

Reluctant

'I am very unwilling to comment on Jeremy Corbyn
very unwilling indeed
and everyone knows that my loyalty to the Party
is unmatched
my record in government stands for itself
and as I say
I am very, very unwilling to comment on Jeremy Corbyn
but seeing as you ask me
and seeing as you've twisted my arm
to get me on to the radio
and the tv
and reluctant though I am
Yes I can't say how reluctant I am
in fact
I'd have to say that if anyone ever votes for
Jeremy Corbyn
we are heading for something like a nuclear winter:
decades in the dark
decades in the wilderness
decades of disaster
(take your pick which of those "decades"
you'd like to quote me on).
But as I say
I'm very, very reluctant to make any comment
and very, very reluctant to come on air like this...'

Backbench Labour MP

'I am a backbench Labour MP. You may once have seen me on a TV programme about garden paths and why garden paths aren't the way they used to be. I hope so. This week I've been on the TV 14 times, on the radio 13 and a half times, I've been interviewed in the *Daily Mail*, the *Daily Star*, *Metro*, and our local paper, the *Wiffly Mercury*. My point is this: I am not in favour of Jeremy Corbyn. What I'm saying is that I'm not in favour of Jeremy Corbyn. That's what I'm saying. I'm saying it loud and clear. Very loud and very clear. I am a backbench Labour MP. I think we need to go back to when Labour was electable. When Labour was electable we transformed this country from being nasty into one that was nice. We brought the nation together and stood up against tyrants. We need to go back to that and not give in. Stand up and don't give in. That's my firm belief. I am a happily married man with children. Most of the time. I am a backbench Labour MP. Did you see the programme about garden paths? They aren't the way they used to be, are they?'

Flagship

'My position as head of the BBC's flagship politics programme "The Westminster Bubble" has come into question. I am proud of my involvement in grassroots politics right from when I was a young man. I and my sister were members of "Tory Tyros" – an activist youth organisation promoting Tory values. At university, I was member of a Tory student group called "Conservatives Serve" and following that I am very proud to have served under the then Minister for British Values Sir Brampton Bampton KCG as his private secretary, and election agent.

As the now executive producer on "The Westminster Bubble" I fail to see why anyone would question my impartiality, particularly in relation to the recent allegations concerning the "tailor" incident in which we appeared to entrap Jeremy Corbyn into taking the offer of a free suit from one of our intrepid reporters, Michael Rosen.

As I've made clear, this was not in breach of any BBC guidelines. Corbyn clearly needs a new suit and if he appeared to admit that on air and accept the offer, that's a matter for him and his terrorist colleagues to discuss.

My sister is the present Minister for Times Tables. Long may she and they prosper.'

Agendas

Tory agenda re Corbyn:

'This man threatens our positions of gross privilege; revolving door careers; sweetheart deals over taxation, core alliances between the monarchy, the Conservative Party, the Church, the monocultural state, networks of old boy associations, and our relentless drive to remove state provision of anything. So, when we attack him for his haircut, beard, jumper, bike, previous relationships – or anything really, we don't really give a damn about any of that. What we're doing is shoring ourselves up, by trying to ridicule and eliminate this threat to our positions. Privilege, our privilege must be maintained at all costs. If it means being insulting to different parts of the population at different times, that's no problem. Machiavelli was right. It's vital to have sections of the public hating each other. We are the beneficiaries because we stay put that way.'

Centre and centre-right Labour agenda re Corbyn:

'We have no idea whether the Corbyn approach is or is not electable but we will do whatever we can to make sure it's not. Whether we stage a coup now or later is only a matter of timing. We are pretending we are not at war with the membership over this, which we do by talking over the top of their heads to people we kid ourselves are our friends in the media. This is because we have very short memories and can't remember that it was only weeks ago in the pre-Corbyn era, the media savaged every aspect of us, whether that was tripping up on a beach, eating bacon sandwiches, or mucking around with low-band taxation. But we can't remember any of this. What we plan to do is to change the constitution of the Labour Party again, so that we can guarantee our return to the leadership which we are entitled to. If necessary we will do all we can to sabotage Corbyn's efforts to win any elections between now and including the next general election.'

Mainstream

I've applied for a job as a mainstream political commentator,
I've written two pieces as examples of what I could write:
they are both about Jeremy Corbyn
on the day before he did the reshuffle.

One of the pieces 'imagines' that Corbyn brings in people from
all sides of the Labour Party
and it condemns him for being weak, dithering, undecided
unable to control the Parliamentary Labour Party
not having the courage of his convictions
and is now the prisoner of some big hitters from the past.

The other imagines that Corbyn has a cabinet made up
largely of people who have been his supporters
and it condemns Corbyn for seizing the levers of power
of surrounding himself with yes men
of creating a mood of fear amongst the more moderate
forces in the party
of behaving like some tin pot South American dictator
or trying to run the Labour Party as if it was his.

How am I doing?

The Polltergeist

The Polltergeist is an imaginary being that appears in pollsters' minds about one week before an election, who 'tells' the pollsters how the outcome of the election is changing every five seconds due to sudden last minute events like how the leader says 'Alright', or eats a bacon sandwich, or what is in some emails, or what the last poll said.

The Polltergeist appears to the pollsters at night so that early in the morning the pollsters can appear on major news outlets with something they call 'News'. After the real election, the Polltergeist returns to its home in Bullshittia where it dies of laughing until it is resurrected by the news outlets in time for the next election.

Brexit Day

On the day we leave the EU

all the foreigners are going to have to leave
and no foreigners are going to come in
and this will mean
we're all going to earn more
and we're going to have more schools
more hospitals,
and more food
we're all going to live in big houses
because all the rich people are
going to give their money away.
They'll say, 'We've got too much money,
you have it.'

On the day we leave the EU

there's going to be no more crime
and no more hooligans
and when it comes to deciding on things like
whether criminals can vote
it's going to be us that decides
because we've got this really good system
where your vote doesn't count if
the person you vote for doesn't get in.
That's what it's going to be like

on the day we leave the EU.

Hours and Hours

The media offer us
hours and hours and hours
of people who say that migrants have made them poor.
Can we please have hours and hours and hours
of them never mentioning the banks crash of 2008
which, in one Tory minister's words 'caused misery to millions';
can we have hours and hours of them never mentioning the
austerity imposed by a government which knowingly
and publicly cut wages;
can we have hours and hours of them never mentioning the
billions sitting in tax havens;
can we have hours and hours of them never mentioning the cost of
wars that achieve nothing
other than causing millions of people to become migrants?
Can we please have media people justifying this sort of stuff
by saying, 'This is what people think' as if there are no
other people who think anything different,
as if they, the media people, have no access to any other forms of
information
which might reveal how we fail to share out the world's resources
in anything like an equitable way,
so that such radio and TV programmes just relay over and over
again
the sound of poor people blaming poor people
over and over and over again.
It's vital that no one ever talks about eyewateringly rich people
divvying up the world's resources for their own benefit.

Why Doesn't the *Sunday Times* Rich List Lead to a Political Revolution?

Every year the *Sunday Times* does us the favour of telling us how the super-rich have got super-richer: the top one thousand and their billions. Even when it's a crisis, says the Sunday Times, it's not a crisis for them.
Even when it's a crisis for you, says the *Sunday Times*, it's not a crisis for them.

I send this information to my friends. We tweet it. We Facebook it. We recycle it as damning info, evidence that this is how capitalism works, an argument for showing that all this talk of benefit dependency or the deficit or 'balancing the books' are a smokescreen for a system that creates inequality. This is not the *Big Issue* saying this. Or *Socialist Worker*. Or *Socialist Revolutionary Worker*. Or *Revolutionary Worker Socialist*. It's the *Sunday Times*.

The *Sunday Times* must be so confident that we'll do nothing. Maybe moan a bit. Write a really angry poem perhaps.
Is it because in the end we think this is how it has to be?
That it's the best way to divvy things up?
Or that it's the only way?
Or that trying anything else would be too risky and would end up with prison camps and starvation?
So in the meantime we should just carry on doing what we do, knowing that everything any politician says about fairness, justice and equality is complete hooey?
Or is it that people think we aren't strong enough or clever enough to change anything or run things ourselves?
Or are we each so in debt that we don't dare defy anyone in case we get thrown out of our homes?
Or that we so long for things in the shops that even when we can't afford them we want to hang on till next week, next month, next year, next decade... when we might just possibly be able to afford it?

Or is it that we're all in a race which any of us could win so we'd better not do anything that might stop the race, even though there will only be a tiny handful of winners, who will only be winners because the rest of us are in the race, doing the running, doing the work, that makes those tiny few the winners anyway?

Everyone Else

They pay for an education
that teaches them that they are
better than everyone else.
They live in enclaves
that separate them off from
everyone else.
They buy health treatment
so that they don't have to be
in waiting rooms and hospitals
with everyone else.
They are driven about in cars
so that they don't have to travel
with everyone else.
They arrive in Parliament
to rule over
everyone else.
They sit in rows baying and jeering
at PMQs
at the letters sent in by
everyone else.
They sit in rows baying and jeering
at PMQs
at the kinds of clothes worn
by everyone else.

The Liberal Elite

1 There are elites in society.

2 Very few of them are liberal.

3 Non-liberal elites tend to run the show.

4 When people say that they are against the 'liberal elite' we
   might hope that the media will ask them
   a) if they are against elites in general or just liberal ones
   b) is the person complaining a member of an elite, and if
      so, what kind?

We Hate Elites

Farage, Le Pen, Trump and May
o how they hate elites
no elites for them
they are the new revolutionaries
they are the new egalitarians
in no-elites Britain
there'll be no super-rich elites
no banking elites
no Oxbridge elites
no elites of experts
no old boy network elites
no inherited wealth elites
no old school tie elites
no private education elites
it's going to be an elite free zone

Money

Money has no passports.
It whizzes across borders
untroubled by journalists or politicians
not noticing it
closing industries,
ending jobs.

C'mon Everybody

C'mon everybody
let's do the politicians' stomp.
They're putting on a show
it's 'Farce dressed as pomp'.

First they're gonna give us
what they call a referendum;
but they don't tell us about
a kind of addendum
where they make up stuff
how it's gonna be hell
if the other side wins
though we know very well
if the other side wins
they get a job on Monday
selling the opposite
of what they said on Sunday.

C'mon everybody
it's the politicians' stomp.
They're putting on a show
it's 'Farce dressed as pomp'.

Then they have an election
to choose the Prime Minister
You don't do the electing
but it's nothing sinister
it all comes down
to a choice between two.
Don't look shocked
it's something new
where the one who drops out
hands the job to the winner
one person one vote:
it's over before dinner.

C'mon everybody
it's the politicians' stomp.
They're putting on a show
'Farce dressed as pomp'.

In the bad old days
we had the aristocracy
now it's so much better
with this kind of democracy.
Meanwhile over
on the other side
they've got a whole new idea
'bout how to decide:
they're very afraid
there's someone's gonna win
so strike off the name:
Jeremy Corbyn.

C'mon everybody
they want us to stomp
to the beat of the show
'Farce dressed as pomp'.

And we are supposed
to love this stuff.
when truth to tell
we've had more than enough
we're not in awe
of the mystique of power;
for millions watching this,
the dream's gone sour.
We know you rushed to war
stopping inspections
now you want our support
in winning elections???!!!

C'mon everybody
we can stuff this stomp
we can see what it is:
'Farce dressed as pomp'.

Wealth Creators

What is it with all this 'wealth-creators' stuff?
Who do they mean when they say, 'wealth-creators'
and what do these 'wealth-creators' do?
And what do they mean by wealth?
So the people who own those businesses, are they really 'wealth-creators'?
If, let's say, I had half a million quid and I decided to start a business making wodgets, and these wodgets sold really well, would I really have 'created wealth'?
If it was just me who 'created wealth' what are all the people making the wodgets and selling the wodgets for me doing? All the people in the offices doing all the paperwork?
Are they creating wealth, or just grateful that I'm 'giving them a job'?
I mean, if we were on a desert island, would they be hanging about, stark naked, not knowing what to do, until I came along and said, 'I've created some jobs for you to do?'
Once you've done these jobs, I'll give you some money and you can go and buy a hut to sleep in. Or would they figure out that they could make a hut without me creating a job for them to do?

Now, of course people come up with great ideas and they contribute to the national or world wealth. But surely they only become stuff we can use or enjoy when people make them.
And surely the way that these things get made is really
just a way for the people who own those businesses to make profits. That is, after they've paid out for raw materials and rent, 'investment' and wages, they get income from sales. The aim of business is to make much more in sales than the total of what they've paid out. So, all the people working for wages, get much less pay for their work, than the owners of the business get in net profit (after they paid out in raw materials, rent, investment and wages). This, society says, is 'fair enough'.

It means, of course, that the waged people in a business don't get back the full value of their combined work. The owners – many of whom may have done absolutely nothing – get a chunk of that value of the work. Some of the ones who do absolutely nothing are the 'shareholders'. They just may be people who wondered what to do with a stack of money they found themselves with. This too is 'fair enough' under the system.

Meanwhile, a great slew of people make 'wealth' by selling and servicing debt. They don't actually make or distribute anything. They just rely on people needing or wanting cash. So they lend money and get interest back on what they lend.

These too are in theory 'wealth creators'. But again, they don't actually 'create' anything. They just milk the people borrowing, many of whom are themselves trying to get profit from other people's work, through their business.

So, we live in a time where we are locked into thinking that a whole range of people who don't actually make or do anything fundamentally useful are worshipped. We are kidded into thinking that they are all immensely clever inventors like Dyson and his Dyson cleaner when in fact, loads of them are nothing of the sort. And even Dyson couldn't make his cleaners without thousands of people making them for him. He'd be stuck on his own at home looking at his fantastic drawings.

But we have lost the language for saying these things. We are stuck inside a language that speaks of 'wealth creators' as only meaning people who employ others. The rest of us should just be eternally grateful that such people are doing this for us. And be bewildered when it occasionally occurs to us that when it comes to the totting up at the end of the year, these 'wealth creators' get richer and richer and the other kind of 'wealth creator' (those who make the stuff or distribute or service it) are squeezed more and more.

Message from a Helpful Rich Person

Hello poor people.
You need to show restraint.
You need to allow your wages
to be controlled.
This is because
you will become better off by becoming poorer.
This will also involve me
becoming richer.
Good people are very rich.
We give you your job.
We do this because we are kind.
It also makes us very rich
but that's just a side effect
you don't need to worry about.

Greece: Stand by for Elder Statesmen with Stuffed Wallets…

Stand by for long grey files of Europe's elder statesmen,
their wallets stuffed with the riches
of bad banking, offshore deals and weird arrangements
we know not of,
standing solemnly in front of us
telling us that the Greek people
are mad, irresponsible,
and don't understand money.
Stand by for them to tell us that the system
is essentially good and the Greek people
are essentially bad,
standby for them to tell us that their core belief
that money can create money is
wise and wonderful
and that the wicked Greek people
are betraying the law of nature
that whatever is lent must be given back
a hundredfold
and the law of nature that trees produce olives
is as nothing compared to that.

Trust Me

'Today I will tell the people
how people are bad for people.
I will them that when they see people on the move
they should be afraid.
I will tell them to trust me.
I will tell them to trust me with money.
I know how good it is.
I will tell the people that money is good.
I will tell them that I know how to handle people and money.
I will tell them that people will be stopped at the border.
Money can move how it wants.
I like it to be known that people with money are good.
I will not talk about money moving out.
I know that money moving out is not good.
I know that money moving out is bad for people.
But I won't say that.
I will only talk about people moving
and how bad that is.
People will listen to me
and will like me.
I will become powerful.
And people with money
will say I am good.'

Song of Trump

My wealth will make you feel better;
the more you hear how rich I am
the more you will love me
the more you will be sure that I am the man
to clean out those who have made you poor.
I will display my gold, come to my tower
see how my suits and shirts conceal the way
my body stores more calories in a day
than you consume in a week;
the bigger I am the better you feel;
you think you are safe in my hands
because I point the finger at wicked people
who steal your wealth
most of whom are poor and foreign;
I identify other rich people who are your enemy,
I say they are an elite
as if I am not and never have been a member of an elite.
I make elite sound dirty even as I flaunt the trappings
of the elite I belong to
because my elite will save you.
Just by walking past my tower
you will feel ten feet tall.
My words about greatness will pump you up
and feel proud to be alive.
At long last you will feel better than someone else.
You will be able to wear me in your heart
like a patriotic pace-maker
and if you're lucky at some not too distant point
I will send you, or one of your children, or any relative
somewhere where they can lock up or deport someone
or go to another country and kill people.
This too will make you feel better
or even great.
Look at my tower.
Feel good.

Trump Tower

Not many people know that Trump Tower is a kind of people's palace
free for everyone, where no elites go,
where people can just walk in and get their country back.
Elites aren't allowed in, because everyone in Trump Tower is kind of equal,
it's a 'we're all in this together kind of place'
where at long last we're being heard
and we don't have to bow down and say nice stuff
about immigrants, blacks, women, or the disabled,
so we're free of all that stuff in Trump Tower
in fact, it's a kind of free place, a free for all,
and Mexicans can't get into it either
and finally all those elites who didn't take notice of us
have had to take it that we're in charge now
and
Mr Trump
we've put him there
he's one of the people
one of the ordinary guys
not one of the elites
and he's in charge of the people's palace
which is why we're free.

Solutions

I wake up this morning to Donald Trump
saying that Muslims shouldn't be allowed into the US
and Toby Young saying that those who don't want Britain
to be officially Christian should leave.
In France, Marine Le Pen rises and rises saying
France for the French.

In the past, our rulers and their supporters had a great urge
to redraw the map. They took out their pens
and moved borders and frontiers;
they drew lines in the sand.
They created countries where they didn't exist before
and put kings and presidents in power in countries far away
from ours
and these kings and presidents
would willingly accept whatever we suggested
by way of raw materials coming out
and our finished goods going in.
We created 'spheres of influence'
and 'strategic interests'
which our commentators refer to today
as if these are unquestionable facts,
as if we are entitled to have these 'spheres of influence'
and 'strategic interests' wherever we want to.

In the middle of the twentieth century
some rulers remembered that old tradition
of moving millions of people from one part
of the earth to another,
or arriving somewhere and eliminating
all who lived there.
Why not do that sort of thing right where we live? they
thought
and millions were moved or killed.

The world woke up in 1945
and decided that this was probably not a good idea.

For some, in the here and now
that 1945 view seems a bit previous:
they are saying now:

'Those people in 1945 were jumping the gun.
Surely there is something to be said
for conjuring up solutions which involve
standing on a traffic island
directing the flow of people:
you leave, you stay, you go, you come,
and this is how we can preserve what is fine
and good about our nation.'

We all like what is fine and good
though we may not necessarily connect it with
this thing called 'nation'.
Especially if this thing called 'nation'
was itself involved at times
in those old habits of moving millions,
and eliminating millions
for the benefit, supposedly,
of that nation.

I mean, the point is surely not that
a nation is itself what is fine and good
(even when it's being foul and bad)
but that we try to find what is fine and good
for everyone.

But, hey, that is so 1945.

Events

Human events may or may not proceed according to physical laws of cause and effect (e.g. I let go of a stone, it drops).

I tend to think that human events proceed according to a more complicated process in which human behaviour is in a permanent state of 'influencing each other' (mutual influence, or reflexive influence).

We see this in language. When I speak to you, part of the reasons for what I say and how I say it is in my awareness of who you are. My behaviour, then is already reflexive. Then you reply, being aware of who I am, whilst being affected by what I said. Cause and effect doesn't describe this fully.

Why am I saying this?

Because the terrible events in Paris raise the spectre of cause and effect thinking. I don't believe that either saying 'ISIS caused the events' or 'the wars caused ISIS' are sufficient explanations of the processes that led to those men massacring those people. We should even be wary of saying that e.g. because a particular interpretation of Islam is a necessary condition for the ISIS mentality that this is a sufficient one. Same goes e.g. that because the wars are a necessary condition for the growth of ISIS that they are sufficient.

In other words, clearly we have lived in a time of 'reflexive influence'. Aha, say some, but this reflexiveness is not symmetrical. That's to say, one side of the question has more power than the other: so, some have implied that 'Islam' is the most powerful side of the process. Not so, say others, it's the wars and the might of the West. I agree, we have to get our relative powers sorted out in this too.

Perhaps, the most telling comment of all was Hollande saying that it was an 'act of war'. Somewhere in the reasons for him saying this, was an awareness that this deed was part of a long war in which many parties over the long history of relations between 'the West' and the 'Middle East' have justified their actions for many different reasons. But at the heart of it, is the use of weapons to kill other human beings. In a terrible way, Hollande clarified that. Surely he entitled us to review this matter as a piece of terrible military history, in which for the most part the greater power was, has been and still is in the hands of the West.

War is a classic case of reflexive influence, ('arms race'), and surely now, after Hollande's words, no Western leader can pretend that if ISIS kill again it isn't part of this war being waged by both sides. In military terms, it really doesn't matter very much what ISIS say to justify what they're doing, or what the West say to justify what they're doing. We can notice it, but we shouldn't be too seduced by it.

Once we have that in our heads, we can ask
1) is either side's war justifiable?
2) millions of people have been killed in this long war, so it's urgent that we find a way to stop it going on... so does it look as if either side killing more people will stop more killing? (And yes, we have noticed that the great majority of people killed in this war are civilians.)

Sporting Nationalisms

If you're from England,
you are supposed to support England,
when England are knocked out or not represented,
you support other parts of the UK
(think Andy Murray but if it's England V Scotland you hate
Scotland),
if other parts of the UK are not represented,
you support Ireland (though obviously at other times Ireland
should be hated and/or despised).
If Ireland are not represented,
you support Europe (though that is where Jonny foreigner comes
from except during the Ryder Cup when he can be good at
beating the USA).
If Europe are not represented,
you support 'the Northern Hemisphere' as in the rugby.

The Northern Hemisphere? I'm supposed to be a northern
hemisphere chauvinist?

I'm not sure where 'we' are supposed to go after that.

An Incredible Discovery

I want to announce tonight an incredible discovery:
A piece of writing that is definitely by Shakespeare,
from one of the history plays.
Scholars are working on it even now.
It's only a short passage.
and it ends rather abruptly.
but I couldn't resist bringing it to you.
I've copied it out word for word.
The speaker seems to be someone with the name Campbell:

My lords, welcome to this goodly tavern
here in hiding can we make plans tonight
you Mandelson, Jowell, Kinnock and Reid
remember though our hands be drenched in blood
from wars too foul to mention now or ever
we can rely on goodly Portland Place
to gloss o'er what crimes we e'er commit
instead will they invite us – or Jack Straw
to give wise counsel on matters more grave:
how what's noble is betrayed by Corbyn
he, like the worm who doth dig deep inside
the holy sepulchre that's our party
bringing withal a multitude, a mob
a swinish troop of people, old and young
who dare to say our place in history
is sullied by that war we do not mention.
We, great lords, who speak for the nation
yea though of late undermined cruelly
by this foolish soft-cheeked smooth-tongued Chilcot
and tonight, my lords, forsooth must we swear
an oath to remove yon upstart Corbyn,
yea, by any means, be they fair or foul.
Were we not set up above the people
as Lords and Barons and Baronesses
to tell the people what is best for them
and place at the helm a golden eagle –

[*Here the manuscript is torn*]

Back in the Room with Blair

You know that moment when hypnotists on TV say
'And... you're back in the room'?
And the people who were hypnotised
don't remember anything of what they saw or did?
It's like that with me and Tony Blair.
He comes on TV and the moment I see his face
and hear his voice, it's as if he's just said,
'And you're back in the room.'
and I've forgotten all about the dodgy dossier
I've forgotten all about the war in Iraq
I've forgotten all about the deaths
he is just
saying really interesting things about
how good it all was when he was in charge.
I look at him and think,
'I'm back in the room...
and whatever he said was the problem with Iraq
it's better there now
and whatever he might say is the problem with anywhere
in the world
will be better if we drop bombs on it,
I'm back in the room
and ready to listen to him,
I'm back in the room.

Letter to My MP

I'm one of your constituents and Labour-voting supporters. I am writing to you to urge you to vote against bombing Syria. My reasons are as follows.

1. Any bombing will kill civilians. Apart from the human tragedy this involves it will also act as a recruiting sergeant for ISL.
2. It is comparatively easy for ISL to hide from aerial bombing, regroup and pose as great resistance fighters to the colonial, imperial and/or corrupt West.
3. There is no proper co-ordinated thought-through strategy of facing the threat that ISL poses. Bombing will make matters worse. There are hardly any examples of aerial bombing being successful – London Blitz, Dresden and Vietnam spring to mind as spectacularly unsuccessful ones.
4. There are alternatives: e.g. putting pressure on the Saudis to prevent them from supporting surrogates and allies of ISL, putting pressure on Turkey to stop buying the oil and to stop bombing the Kurds, helping to create a regional conference(s) in order to discuss peaceful solutions.
5. There is a real danger that escalating the conflicts through bombing will bring on the danger of world war. We should be making it a priority to de-escalate.
6. It's a good time to question why the UK is involved at this kind of level in foreign conflicts. Is there any cogent, rational explanation as to why the UK is involved in the Middle East acting as policeman, assailant and judge while, on occasions posing as mediator and arbitrator. It seems to be either a hangover from colonial times and/or part of the UK tail being wagged by the US dog. I would suggest that every time the UK is called upon to support the US or another country's foreign adventures, the Conservatives are able to present themselves as the real true 'defenders' of the UK. The exception is of course Iraq which very few now would take exception to calling a blunder, a tragedy and one of the reasons why we now face armed Islamism in many parts of the world. If for no other reason, opposing the bombing of Syria is one way we can put some distance between social democratic politics and the bombing of the Middle East.

Why We Should Go to War...

'We can drop bombs through the eye of a needle.
We can't always find the needle.
But we drop the bombs anyway.
And they land very accurately.
On, er... whatever's there.
Which is good, isn't it?

There will be civilian casualties.
That's true.
But these will be less important than our civilian casualties.
I think we're all agreed on that.

Every time a bomb falls out of one of our planes
onto the people of the Middle East,
our credibility with the people of the Middle East goes up.
We will strain every tissue to bring people
together to discuss how to bring an end to the killing
apart from the killing we're doing.
And the people of the Middle East
are with us on this.
They're always very grateful to us.
They love us.
And always have done.
All the way back to... er... Kitchener..
and Gordon.
Great men. Much loved.

We are very sympathetic to the
plight of the refugees.
Yes, there will be refugees
as a result of our bombing action
we know that,
but you can rely on us
to... er... send them back,
where we will bomb them.
You can rely on us to do that.

I would like to make a point about Russia.
We don't trust Russia.
They say they're killing ISIS people.
If they are, they're doing it in the wrong way.
If they're not, they should be.
Yes.

And Assad.
Assad is the most evil person to have ever
walked the earth.
He kills innocent civilians.
Can you imagine that?
We are doing all we can to
remove his enemies from the face of the earth.
That's what we're doing
and we know why we're doing it.
And none of us want the Russians in there
instead of us.

A quick point about Jeremy Corbyn.
He may look like a weak, useless, pacifist.
And he is.
He is very, very weak.
Very, very useless.
And very, very pacifist.
He's also a crazed killer.
Incredibly dangerous.
And with the potential to bring Britain to its knees
in the blink of an eye.

He and his evil Marxist henchmen
sympathise with terrorists.
I can put my hand on my heart
and say we on this side of the argument
have never ever sympathised
with terrorists anywhere.
You will know for example
that we have never in anyway
ever ever had anything to do with
Northern Irish Protestant paramilitaries
directly, indirectly, through intermediaries
or secretly through our secret services.
Never. Ever. Not ever. Or ever.

Nor any terrorists in Libya.
Or in Syria.
Oh, no Syria is different.
Sorry, as you were.
In Syria we sympathise with moderate terrorists.
Who do their terrorism moderately.
There are about 70,000 of them.
The moment we bomb ISIS
the 70,000 moderate terrorists will come
rushing out of their houses and
head for Assad and get him.
There may be some Russians in the way.
Yes.
We have figured that out.
But... er... we haven't figured out what to do about that yet.
But the 70,000 moderate terrorists
will get that sorted.
Russia isn't the big bear it once was.
No, really it's just an old threadbare teddy.
A thread*bear*.
Sorry, for that levity in a moment of deep, deep seriousness.

Which reminds me:

No government takes the decision lightly to go to war...
that's why we keep doing it again and again
er... not lightly.
So, I would like to plead with you
to stay united with us on this.
After all, there's no one else out there who's united.
Thank you.
Vote for war.
We've got to keep this economy going somehow.
Keynes wasn't right.
But Keynes for killing makes sense.
Pump prime the arms economy, stimulated growth.
You see, everything connects.
When it doesn't connect, there's trouble.
And when there's trouble we pour oil on troubled waters.
Oil? Who mentioned oil?
Not me.
You must be thinking of someone else.
Thank you.
Bombs away!
Chin chin.'

Dangerous

'As a long standing Labour Party member
who was proud to have supported the invasion of Iraq
I would like to alert you to the dangers of
Stop the War.
They are a dangerous, murderous group.
I deeply resent the fact that some people
in Stop the War say that I am part of some
dangerous, murderous group when all I ever
did was vote for the invasion of Iraq.
I can see no connection between the invasion of Iraq
and being dangerous or murderous.
The Stop the War people on the other hand
have a direct link with being dangerous and murderous.
You can tell it from the name:
Stop the War.
There, that says it all, doesn't it?
That's why we must stand together
and fight for a safer, stronger Britain.'

Response to the War Party

Whatever they say about us,
we haven't killed anyone.
They've killed hundreds of thousands.
Hundreds and hundreds of thousands.
Hundreds and hundreds and hundreds of thousands.
Perhaps they think that if they keep pointing
at us, saying,
'Stop the War are the problem!'
no one will notice the blood
on their hands.

The Civilian

The civilian is sacred
not because they are right
not because they are good.
They may be neither.
The civilian is sacred
because they are alive.

In every war
leaders will explain
why the civilian must die.
They will explain why they are sorry.
They will explain
why the civilian must die.
The civilian must die,
they say,
because there must be a war.
There must be a war, they say,
so that the civilian can be saved
The civilian must die
so that they can be saved.

But:
if the civilian is sacred
there can be no war.

Marxist Horoscope

Today you realise you are born into a world not of your own
choosing.

Later you observe that social being determines consciousness
and not the other way round.

At work you discover that the sum total of what people are
paid is less than the value of what's produced.

Glancing at your bills you realise a large proportion of your
income is spent on paying interest on what you have
borrowed.

Watching TV it occurs to you that a tiny minority own and
control most of the worlds resources, and means of
producing.

As you think about the world you see that most people can
only earn a living by selling their ability to work.

In a bus passing a bank you see that a tiny minority make
money through rent, profit and interest.

A newspaper reminds you that the dominant ideas are ideas
that suit those who own and control nearly everything.

Everyone tells you, you are alone but in order for things to be
made and sold, you are brought together with others.

Thinking of your school days you remember that your
teachers were once themselves taught.

Listening to my Mother

I am listening to my mother
she's knitting
knitting needles clicking

I am listening to my mother
she's sewing
sewing machine humming

I am listening to my mother
she's typing
typewriter clacking

I am listening to my mother
in my head.

For Eddie

The silence after lasts forever.
It is as quiet in the second it ended
as it is years later.
Quieter than a painting.
There is nothing as quiet as this.
It is as quiet as nothing.